Meditatio

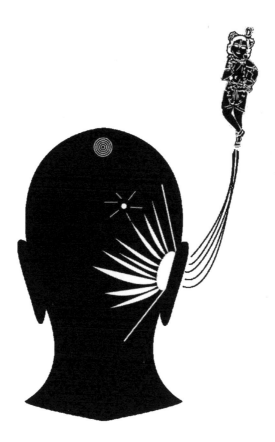

Michael Beloved

Meditation Pictorial

Initial Scanning:
- Bernard Adjodha

Rough manuscript diagrams:
- Marcia K. Beloved, Sharon Thornton

Cover Art + Final diagrams:
- Michael Beloved

Graphics Editor + Lord Shiva Art:
- Sir Paul Castagna

Proof-reading editor:
- Dear Beloved

Financial Outlay
- Bernard Adjodha

Correspondence   **Email**
Michael Beloved   axisnexus @gmail.com
3703 Foster Ave
Brooklyn NY 11203 USA

ISBN
978-0-9819332-2-1
LCCN
2009902672

Editorial appreciations

This book was produced after 35 years of solid continuous painstaking practice and verification experiences. I am obligated to my wife, Marcia K. Beloved, who drew many of the original diagrams, tested many of the procedures and proof-read this edition. Our appreciations are also due to Sharon Thornton, the mother of my eldest daughter. She assisted with formatting and drawing for many of the early manuscripts of this book. Her good will, dedication and loyalty cannot be repaid by me.

Last but not least, is the artist and psychologist, Sir Paul Castagna. His comments and reviews of many of our books served to provide much needed objectivity in this realm of near total subjectivity which is the spiritual quest.

Table of Contents

4

Teacher Appreciations

We honor these persons who contributed to the realizations in this book:

Lobsang T. Rampa, Śrī Ramana Maharshi of Arunachala, Arthur Beverford, his spiritual master Rishi Singh Gherwal, Yogi Harbhajan Singh, Paramhansa Yogānanda, Śrī Yukteshvar Giri, Lahiri Mahāśaya, Bābāji of the Kriyā lineage, Acharya Gambhiranatha, B.K.S. Iyengar, Swāmī Sachidananda, Yogacharya Swāmī Kripalvananda, Swāmī Yogeshwarananda Saraswati, Śrīla Bhaktivedānta Swāmī, Mahādeva Shiva, Śrī Balarām and Śrī Krishna.

Lobsang T Rampa

He did much to publicize reincarnation. He wrote in clear and simple terms, stressing the opening of the third eye and development of psychic perception.

Arthur Beverford

He was a disciple of Rishi Singh Gherwal, who translated the Hatha Yoga Pradipika and parts of the Mahābhārata. We were given an opportunity to study some of Guruji Gherwal's books during 1970-1973 and some of them are still in print. He was one of the first Indians to write a book in English about yogic feats in India. According to Yogi Beverford, his teacher's books were used as the basis for Spalding's Masters of the Far East and may have inspired Yogānanda's Autobiography of a Yogi.

Harbhajan Singh Mahayogin

He did much to help drug-oriented American youths. He publicized the bhastrika prāṇāyāma method which is known as breath-of-fire. This is a quick method for mastering the vital force of the body. I studied under some of his prominent disciples in the years of 1972-1974. Yogi Bhajan showed me the brain breath which may instantly cleanse the mind of lower ideas and free one from dreams in the lower regions. In my opinion Yogi Bhajan's breath technique is the sure method for purifying and raising kundalini.

Paramhansa Yogānanda Mahayogin

He did much to publicize Indian mysticism. He attracted many Westerners to meditation and samādhi trance consciousness. His books influenced thousands of Westerners to pursue yoga practice. He did not divulge methods in his books but his processes were divulged through initiation.

Yukteshwar Giri

He was the spiritual teacher of Yogānanda. Lahiri Mahāśaya was their predecessor. In the year 1973 I took help from Yogi Yukteswar. This was done on the astral plane since he was not available physically. He taught me certain meditation techniques.

Lahiri Mahāśaya

This great yogin showed me the system of opening the orbital lalāta chakra which shines and gyrates like a miner's light at the central top of the forehead. He gave me some other key processes and asked me to write extensively. He stressed the mulabandha rechanneling for celibacy.

B.K.S. Iyenkar Mahāyogin

His *Light on Prānāyāma* is an exceptional and authoritative book. It proves conclusively that a determined yogi can perfect the process. Though he was embodied at the time, I met him astrally. He showed me the process of cleansing the *āpana* energy out of the solar plexus area and replacing it with *prāṇā*. When I asked him about the necessity for *prāṇāyāma* in comparison to the religious process of chanting holy names, he explained, "I worship Hanumānji. He is my favorite deity. Tendencies from previous lives continue. In the *Gītā*, this is established, where the Blessed Lord Krishna stated that in the next human birth, the aspiring yogi continues his former practice. I also chant holy names. Hanuman empowered me with this yoga process. It is a residual effect from previous lives."

Swāmī Sachidananda

He founded Integral Yoga. He was gracious enough to show me what occurs in the body when the kundalini energy efficiently passes through all nerves and tissues. I never met him physically. Our contact was astral only. He did however give me some valuable techniques. In particular, he showed the jalandhar neck centering lock where the chin is drawn back for an adjustment whereby the life force passes efficiently through the spine into the brain. He was fatherly in relation to me.

Swāmī Kṛpalvānanda

This Yogācārya who wrote *Science of Meditation*, showed me many techniques in the meditation process. He stressed the cleansing of the imput and output air energy channels. It was from him and from Swāmī Yogeshwarananda that I took the hint of cleansing the lower trunk of the body, for unless this is properly aligned, one cannot consolidate yoga practice.

Swāmī Yogeshwaranda Saraswati

He wrote *Science of Soul*, which gives valuable information about the meditation process. He showed me the location and range of the spontaneous sound current. He revealed the importance of a firm spine and explained and revealed the third eye gap, a space between the eyebrows, which is located by horizontal and vertical beam sweeps of energy.

Śrīla Bhaktivedānta Swāmī

I am indebted to my Vaishnava spiritual master, Śrīla Bhaktivedānta Swāmī, who gave volumes of information in numerous books which are primarily devoted to devotional service to Lord Krishna. Some of his purports elaborate on yoga.

Mahādeva Shiva

My respects are due to this greatest of the yogis. He insisted that I write down something about the hereafter. In fact, all the information provided on that subject was inspired into the mind of the writer by him. His assistance to the writer cannot be repaid in any measure.

Lord Balarāma

This deity instructed me that in matters pertaining to this book I should consult with Mahādeva Shiva. He said to me, "My dear boy, go to Mahādeva. He is the master of the yogis. No yogi is greater than him. Whatever you need to know about yoga you may learn from him."

Lord Krishna

This Blessed Lord assisted me considerably throughout the years. Every step of progress was acquired with His assistance and subtle guidance. He directed me in how to be submissive to various authorities, even to arrogant and somewhat misguided ones. He assisted in the dream clarity portion of this book. He told me that unless one comes to the stage of perceiving the actions in the dream world and clearly realizing that place as being another territory, it is doubtful that one could learn the hereafter geography. He recommended a careful study of His Bhagavad Gītā and Uddhava Gītā discourses.

Introduction

Meditation can be learned if one is patient with the psyche and conducts at least two sessions per day. The mind developed its own habits. Therefore one should patiently restrain it. Habit is the nature of the mind and thus one can use the habit procedure to train it. Regular meditation at a set time daily is the method of indoctrinating the mind.

Read through this book casually at first. On the second reading begin to practice the exercises. If a procedure is difficult, practice the easy parts for a time and then gradually adopt the more difficult techniques.

Beginners will do better if meditation takes place under favorable conditions. Usually silence is required. The place should be of subdued lighting or pitch dark. There should be adequate ventilation. Some beginners may be facilitated by pleasant music.

Be persistent. Keep notes of realizations and experiences.

Meditation is the gateway to perceiving the components of the psyche. Such perception causes psychic experiences which verify for the self its survival beyond the physical body.

Chapter 1 begins with the most basic meditation technique of third eye focus and techniques to direct the energy and focus awareness within the mind. As meditation improves, so will one's focus on dreams. Tips for dream clarity are included as well as a final note on indications of an opened third eye.

Chapter 2 reveals how to still the mind's problems and introduce clarity of thought.

In order to further advance in meditation, one should pay close attention to Chapter 3 which addresses sex and the bodily chakras.

After covering fundamentals in the first three chapters, the next part through Chapter 7 introduces advanced techniques for focused meditation, followed by a primer on dreams.

Chapters 9 and 10 tackle the moment of death and aspects of the life force.

The last four chapters cover a broad range of topics of great interest to those who are advancing in meditation. Topics range from cross-world travel and sensual energies to open-eye meditation and departed souls. In a sense, the first half of this book walks through techniques for beginner and advanced meditation. The second half transitions to a discussion that provides answers to a great deal of questions and solutions to the frustrations that will inevitably arise as you progress.

Chapter 1

Third-eye Focus

This practice trains the mind in focusing into the space between the eyebrows. In the subtle body there is an energy gyration center between the eyebrows. This place is called the brow chakra, as well as the 3rd eye. Śrī Krishna mentioned this location in one verse of the Bhagavad Gītā:

- *...and that meditator who even at the time of death, with an unwavering mind, being connected devotedly, with psychological power developed through yoga practice, and having caused the energizing breath to enter between the eyebrows with precision, goes to the Divine Supreme Person. (Bhagavad-Gītā 8.10)*

How long should you meditate? I recommend two periods of 30 minutes minimum; one in the early morning soon after rising and one in the evening before resting. If you cannot afford 30 minutes, I suggest 15 minutes. If you cannot afford that, I suggest just 5 minutes.

What will you gain from meditation? You will acquire orderliness of the mental and emotional processes. This may not be achieved in a hurry. It may take time. Meditation requires patience with the self.

Procedure

1. Contain all feelings, thoughts and ideas within the skull.

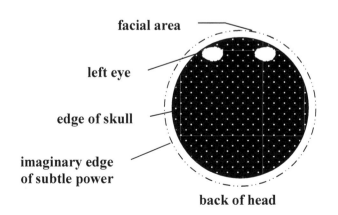

facial area

left eye

edge of skull

imaginary edge
of subtle power

back of head

2. Ignore everything outside the skull.

Observe the speckled darkness in the head. It is all around spherically but is usually noticed in the front only, due to focus orientation through the face of the head.

Withdraw interest in everything outside the skull.

Ask yourself, "Where am I?" Try to locate your identity in the subtle space of intense consciousness.

---

3. Focus on the left eyeball.

4. Switch focus to the right eyeball

---

5. Be aware of both eyeballs as spaces of subtle power.

6. Trace energy in both eyeballs back to the common point where the optic power originates.
To do this, mentally retract the eyeballs; then push them out. That identifies the focusing energy.
Direct the energy backwards from both eyes. Follow it to the vortex.

7. **Origin of Optic Power**

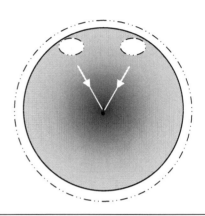

8. Contract the eyelids tightly. Focus into the eyeballs.

9. **Re-assert optic power**

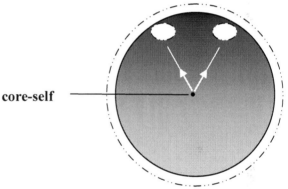

core-self

10. Relax eyelids.
Become aware of the contained mental power surrounding the optic meeting point. *(Dotted lines in diagram indicate partial drainage of soul power.)*

11.

edge of intense soul power

12. Pull eyeballs back into head by will power. In the effort to do this, physical muscles may react to mimic the mental action. Repeatedly do this and practice for some time until the mental action operates without physical response. This practice causes a separation between the physical and psychological.
Intentionally retract the optic power.
Repeatedly attempt this.
Then relax the eyeballs.

13.   **Retract optic power. Focus on intense soul power.**

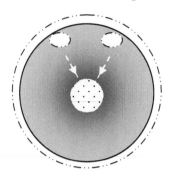

14. Push subtle eyeballs outward by will power only.
Assert mental power through the optic channel to the eyeball.

15.   **Re-assertion of mental force through optic channel**

intense soul power

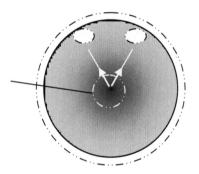

16. Move central power downwards as if energy is draining through an imaginary funnel in the neck.
Question yourself:
Where am I?
Does this energy have a center?

17.   **Downward passage of soul power**

18. Conceive of a flow of energy through the back of the head. Attempt to direct the seeing-focus through that energy flow.

19.

intense soul power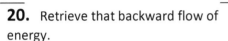

**flow of energy
through back of head**

20. Retrieve that backward flow of energy.
Simultaneously pull in mental power from the front area.

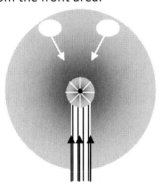

21. Be aware of the intense radiant energy.

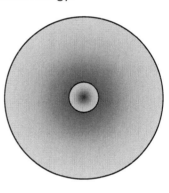

22. Feel the consciousness expanding to fill the skull space.

Loss of intense soul power

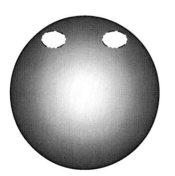

23. Feel soul power expanding outward in all directions.
Spherical field of awareness

24. Reverse the expansion by mentally retracting the energy of consciousness in all directions. Direct it to the intense radiant awareness in the center.

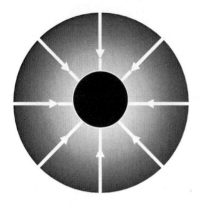

25. Detect the limits of intense consciousness.
Retract consciousness inwards with a stronger pulling focus. Shrink and intensify the consciousness.
Remain in this state for some time.

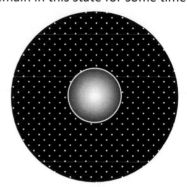

26. Send energy to eyeballs.
Be aware of the origin point of the optic channels. Re-assert optic power.

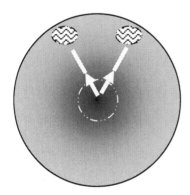

27. With eyes closed, look through the eyeballs to the dark space between the eyebrows.
Focus on that dark space.
Feel the energy moving through subtle circuitry from the optic meeting point through the eyeballs to the space between the eyebrows. If the focus becomes stalled in the eyeballs, make repeated attempts to move it to the dark space between the eyebrows

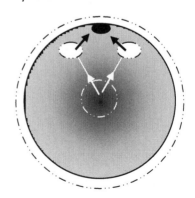

28. Stop the release of energy originating at the optic meeting point. In the state of no-focus, make efforts to determine where you are. Try to locate the I-self in that abstract space of consciousness

29. Locate the eyeballs and trace backwards to the meeting point of the optic force.

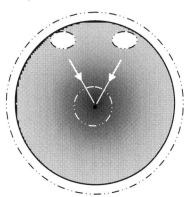

30. Retract the energy of consciousness from all directions, inward. Direct it to the intense radiant awareness in the center.

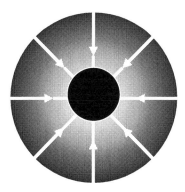

31. Diffuse the central consciousness. Reflect on the vagueness of the mental space. Consider how memories, reasoning ability, emotions, feelings, random imaginations and day dreaming ceased.
How do these mental constructions occur? Can this process be visualized in detail?

32. **Diffusion of subtle power**

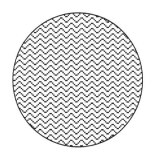

33. Refocus optic channel to darkness at center of eyebrows.

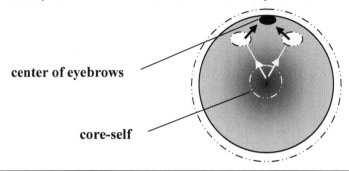

center of eyebrows

core-self

---

34. Gently and willfully withdraw the energy from optic channels and return it to the origin point. Slowly relax the focus.

Fading of optic power

---

35. Send energy directly from the optic meeting point to the darkness between the eyebrows. The dark space between the eyebrows is the location of a subtle or third eye. Keep the focus through that central area

Establishment of singular optic blast

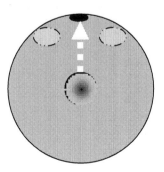

Mental Maneuvers for Subduing the Erratic Mind

1. Focus on the dark space in the frontal part of the head.

2. Focus on the mental space in which thoughts, memories and images appear.

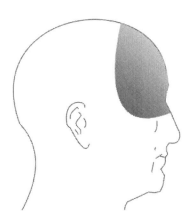

3. Think of whatever comes to mind.

4. Make mental chatter. Say within the mind, "Make efforts to sort mental energy."

Look and listen for a verbal mental response.

My spouse!
My friend!
My bills!

Sort mental energy?

5. Change the view. Pull in the eyeballs by sheer will power; then push out by will power.
Identify the energy in the eyeballs.

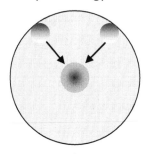

6. Mentally pull in tighter on the eyeballs.

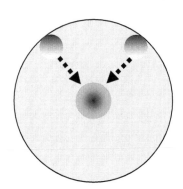

7. Relax eye pressure.
   With physical eyes closed, focus mind in center of eyebrows.
   Use one blast of focus.

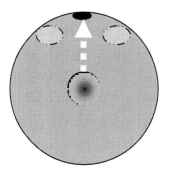

8. Compel the mind to focus on a tiny speck of light.
   Choose a speck among the unlimited number of specks in the mind space before you. Be sure to keep eyes closed. If possible be in a room with subdued light or with pitch-black darkness.

Mystic cloud in facial area

9. The speck of light will be lost soon after the mind focuses on it. The mind may become depressed or may project the feeling of boredom.

Disregarding the mind's negative attitude, select another speck for focus.

When this speck is lost identify another and focus on it.

Do this repeatedly until the mind tires.

When the mind tires choose a small area in the dark mind space. This area may or may not have specks of light. The mind will lose the selected portion of mind space. Select another portion. When the mind tires or loses focus, select another. After this, cease all focus.

---

10. Retreat to the intense radiant awareness center and remain in stillness there. Be conscious of the mental force which surrounds the I-self.

---

11. Focus on the space between the eyebrows.

At first apply much mental pressure.

When this becomes tiring, relax.

After some relaxation, apply gentle forward pressure with a focus between the eyebrows.

Ignore the eyes completely.

With physical eyes closed, send one blast of energy to the center of the eyebrows.

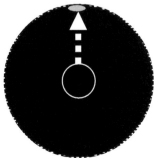

12. Retreat to the intense radiant awareness in the center of consciousness.

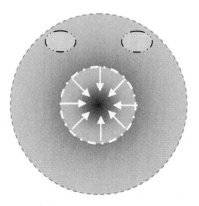

13. Maintain the meditative state.
Lose track of the inner limits of intense soul power.

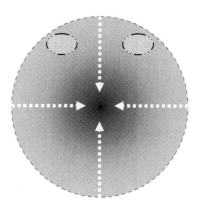

Dream Clarity
<u>To remember dreams, do the following:</u>

- Buy an alarm clock. If you are a light sleeper, use a low-sounding alarm. If you are a sound sleeper, use a loud alarm. You may ask someone to awaken you at a certain time. The person should be given permission to insist that you rise from slumber.
- Set clock to ring exactly five hours after you go to bed. In five hours the body is rested to a degree.
- When the alarm rings, rise to your feet. Turn off the ringer. Go to evacuate the body.
- Return to bedside. Have a pen and notebook ready to record experiences. Write down the ideas, names, places, or feelings that come to mind.
- Do this at every session. Do not be frustrated if there are no memories.
- If no ideas come, simply observe your thinking. Record the thoughts in the journal.
- Talk to the mind:
- "Well, mind. How do you regard this? They say that rising in the middle of the night increases dream recall."
- Mind replies, "This is the worst thing in the world. We were just getting cozy, and besides, I like to be groggy." Tell mind: "We were instructed. Let us apply the advice."
- After doing this for one week, begin a new procedure: Rest on your back with head pulled back, chin raised. This is best done on a firm bed or hard surface.

- In this position, with head tilted back, do the 3rd eye focus.

After the mind tires, relax the head to a normal posture. Do a centralized focus on the core-self.

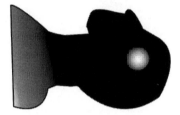

- When you tire or nod out, move to a comfortable posture and continue the third eye or central focus meditation until you fall asleep.
-

Special Notes

- If the alarm is ignored by the mind, and you are unsuccessful in getting up, the alarm is either too low or the mind is too accustomed to the sound. Take one of these steps:
- Buy a clock which has a different alarming sound. Put the clock in a different location to which you must walk to silence the sound.
- Have someone awaken you instead.
- If you awaken before the clock rings, or if alarm rings and you awaken without feeling groggy, do NOT jump out of bed. Stay silent and recall ideas, pictures and memories. Record this in a journal. In the effort to recall, do not allow the mind to jump from one idea to another quickly. Reflect each experience slowly and then record it in writing.
- Make an effort to slow the mind's recording memory system by not paying attention as soon as the mind speeds up its display. As soon as you remove the attention, the mind will slow down the rate of display of images and sounds.

Third-eye Vision

An opened third eye may be indicated by any of the following occurrences in the frontal part of the head:

1. A borderless hazy space

2. A borderless dark blue or purple space

3. An outwardly or inwardly moving blue or purple, grey or brown disc

4. An outwardly or inwardly moving blue or purple ring or shape

5. A five-pointed star

6. An eight-pointed star

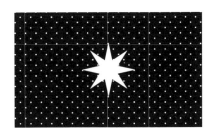

7. An instantaneously appearing star speck

8. A bright yellow, bright green or golden ring

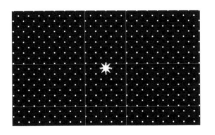

9. A transparent oval shape

10. A transparent rectangular space

11. A transparent round space

12. A scene of an actual earthly place, seen visually through an oval, rectangular or round space

13. A flickering light inside or on the edge of the head

14. A bright flash of light in head

Chapter 2

Clarity of Thinking / The Back of Head

1. Be in a dark room. Focus on the back of head.

2. Locate speckled darkness in front of head.

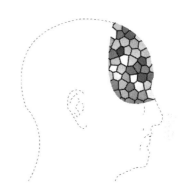

3. Locate dense slightly speckled darkness at the back of the head. This might be non-visual. One might not see but one might feel the darkness.

4. Make a mystic oblong gap at the back of the head to merge inner darkness with outer darkness outside the head. In achieving this one might first try to imagine the gap. Do this repeatedly during meditation for at least seven days.

5. Extend the gap around the top of the head.

6. Remain in the speckled darkness.

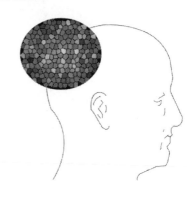

7. Relax the attention. Move the attention to the front of the head. Think of a problem while situated in dense darkness.

8. Think of something you need.

9. Refocus at the back of the head. Try to think of something at the back of the head. It will not be possible to do so unless some attention is shifted to the frontal area.

10. Refocus at the back of the head. That is the normal clarity of consciousness. It is the basic awareness.

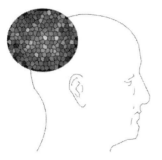

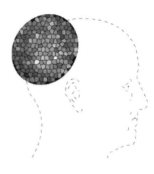

11. Why is it a dense darkness? Can clarity exist in mental darkness?

12. Can spiritual light be seen in darkness?

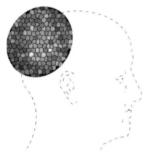

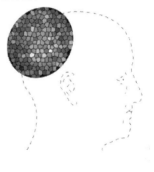

This dense darkness is a type of spiritual light which is not perceived due to unfamiliarity with it and excessive orientation to material sensual light.

Meditate here regularly. Store yourself away here for clarity of mind, for having access to a higher spiritual security, for knowing that your existence is definite, eternal and non-dependent on mundane variety.

Get used to spiritual light which is sometimes perceived as material darkness and which is recognized by the clarity it produces.

Real darkness cannot give clarity of consciousness but rather gives fear and confusion of ideas and objectives.

Disorient the self from over-dependence on mundane variety. Become familiar with spiritual light in the mental darkness at the back of the head.

Problem Removal

1. Think of a problem.

2. Break the energy of it into parts.

3. Isolate the problem energy.

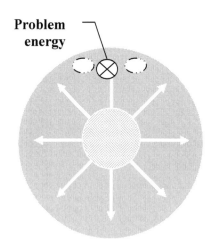

Problem energy

4. Retract the problem energy.

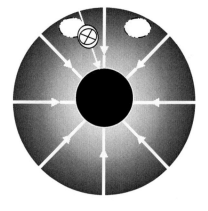

5. Retract all mental energy, including the problem energy, into the central I-self

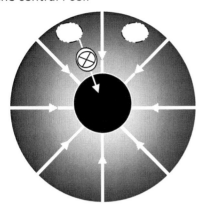

6. Contract or compress the problem energy.

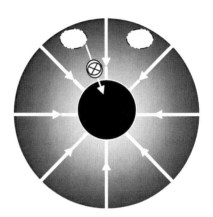

7. Pull in the problem energy further.

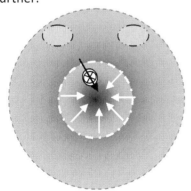

8. While holding the problem energy near to the core-self, lose track of outer limits of consciousness.

9. Pull the problem energy in further.

10. Hold until the problem energy is destroyed by mental force.

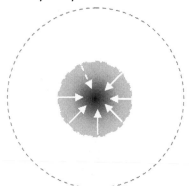

After this session, take notes on whatever comes to mind about the problem. Heed and implement any sensible advisories and suggestions which you discover or which were inspired into your mind.

Naad Sound

The sound current in the head is a segment of the cosmic sound vibration *oṁ*. This is for the convenience of the individual meditator. Some of this sound comes from Lord Krishna's flute and is heard in the head, spreading from the area of the right internal ear.

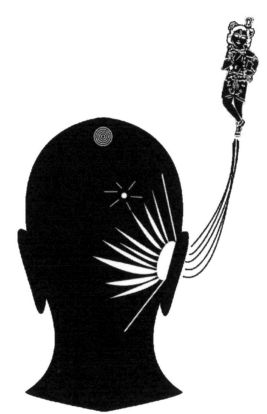

How to meditate on naad sound

1. Sit on a chair, or sit in yoga posture, or lie on your back on a firm surface.

2. Close eyes.

3. Observe darkness behind closed eyes.

4. If you are indoors, close curtains to keep out street light. Darkness is preferred.

5. Observe the general darkness behind the closed eyelids.

Make an attempt to turn around mentally inside the physical head.

If you find you cannot, return to facial orientation. Relax. Make the effort to mentally turn to the back again.

6. Make sure that you place your mind in the dark empty space. That space should be lighter and less dense than the space in the front part of the skull.

The lightness you feel there is real because the back of the head has less compact thought energy than the front. Thoughts do have psychic weight.

Once you put the mind there, settle there. Assess that area.

The darkness is not totally dark, for it has microscopic speckles of light, moving randomly. How is vision possible here? How is any type of perception possible? This is not optic vision. This is energy perception without distinctive, partitioned forms.

This may be termed as a type of *prāṇa* vision, mento-emotional energy perception.

Train the mind to remain in the speckled darkness.

7. If you find that the mind is unsettled, relate to it mentally. The mind may respond. Relate mentally to the mind, thinking, "I prefer this atmosphere. This is a new compartment. We could move out of the crowded cluttered front portion of the skull. We can settle here."

8. Of course, the mind is discouraged by this suggestion. Still, it will consider what was presented. As the mind considers, move your attention to the inner right ear and try to catch the ringing naad sound.

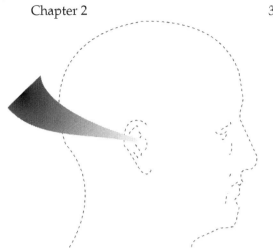

If you still cannot catch it, do this over and over, day after day until you do. Be confident that eventually you will hear it.

Once the sound is caught, use it as your main reference in meditation.

Always go first to the right, upper back of the head.

As soon as you get there, turn and face the inner ear and you will immediately hear the sound.

Keep your attention on this sound for some time. Keep the mind away from the thought-heavy, thought-crowded, weighty, front section of the brain.

9. If your mind remains resistant to and disliking towards this practice, you will struggle with a negative mood. The mind's negativity will affect you by producing a depressed feeling towards this. However, you should persist with patience and tolerance. The negativity is an energy more than it is a mood. The mind is transformed into this energy because it is in unfamiliar territory. It does not perceive any enjoyment from the activity.

As soon as you relax the focus or become absorbed with the negativity, the mind will return to the facial area of the head, where it will again display images and sounds. You will find yourself observing these, responding to these, giving approval or disapproval to these, just as a person who sits in a theatre where a film is shown on a screen.

When you discover yourself in that frontal area, viewing the thought constructions and memories of the mind, question yourself as to how you were relocated, moved as it were, to that frontal part of the head. What moved you? Why did you not notice when you were initially relocated from the back area?

As you reflect on this, turn yourself to the back again and focus there.
Begin the back focus.

You will find yourself in the front again and again. Question yourself about this and refocus on the back. Do this repeatedly.

10.   You will not be able to keep the mind in the back. The mind will be there for a split second and then return to the front. Your attention will follow those movements, just as a wagon follows a horse which is harnessed to it.

If you are not advanced, use the third eye concentration and master the single beam focus (third eye focus) on the third eye location first. That will curb the mind and initiate naad sound focus.

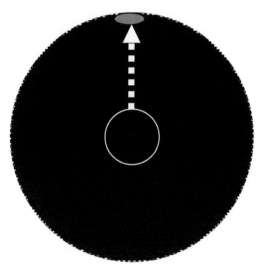

Chapter 3

Sex-prone Body

The sex-prone body is characterized by an overload of carbon dioxide in the lower body of both genders and the breasts of women.

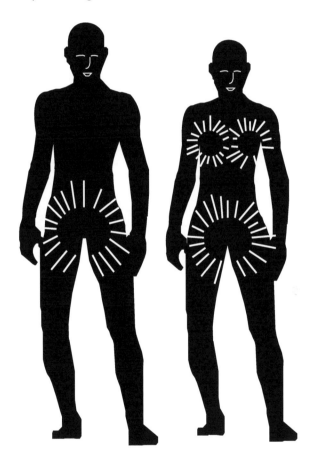

In such a sex-prone body, a minimal quantity of hormone energy rises into the brain. Most of the energy is absorbed by the slow-moving, carbonated blood in the sexual areas.

Due to the overload of carbon dioxide there is a pressure for increased sex participation and that absorbs even more of the life force power by loss of generative fluid, sex hormones and secretions.

Sex-free Body

This contrasts with the situation in which the body is purified by kundalini yoga and vegetarian diet. The lower portion of the body is carbon dioxide free due to full *prāṇāyāma* breathing and/or kundalini yoga with *bhastrik* rapid breathing and body stretching. The highly-oxygenated blood circulates rapidly and replaces carbon dioxide.

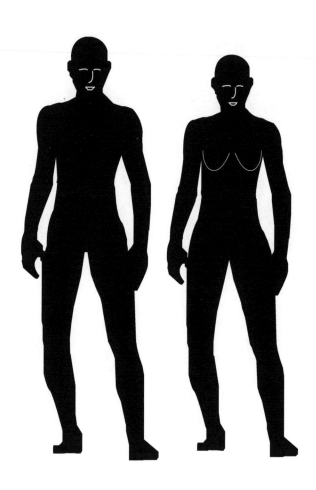

The kundalini energy goes to the brain and is not absorbed by a high concentration of carbon dioxide as in the sex-prone situation.

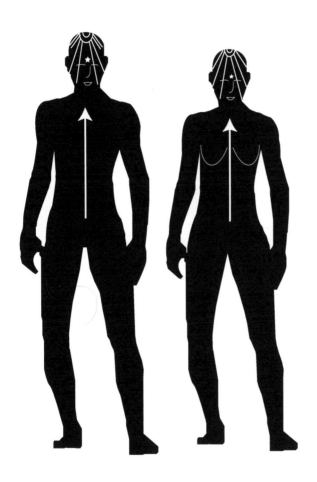

Kundalini Yoga

Celibacy is required

For those who practice kundalini yoga, sexual chastity is absolutely necessary. In fact, for success in the classic ashtanga yoga, celibacy is required. To clean the gross body, a certain type of diet, along with yoga exercises and breath infusion, is required. To purify the subtle or astral body, celibacy with certain breathing exercises is required. Inasmuch as blood travels through the gross body, energizing airs pass through the subtle form. These must be purified by *prāṇāyāma* breathing exercises. The subtle body is nourished by seminal or ovarian auric energies just as the gross body is nourished by natural foodstuffs. Sexual energies should be redirected.

Difficulties with sexual pleasure

The sexual organs are capable of begetting progeny but since these organs are pleasure-yielding, they present a great impediment for those who want success in yoga practice. If there were no pleasure involved in begetting, people who require children would beget and then forget the use of the genitals. Since a pleasure is there, one is prone to indulgence as it is very difficult to forget sexual pleasure. Even yogis become habituated to sex pleasure, so we can just imagine the compulsion of others.

Starved for energy

The tongue is meant for tasting, to certify food values, but if that sense organ tastes continually, or if the soul wants to exploit the tasting duty of the tongue, the stomach and all other parts of the body suffer the consequences. Similarly, if the genitals are greedy for pleasure, the subtle body suffers by depletion of energy.

The actual cause

There are various reasons for sexual over-indulgence and for the most part, the parties involved are usually not the essential cause. It is mainly related to entities requiring rebirth. Due to intoxication with earthly life, pride in having earthly bodies and ignorance of the world hereafter, we simply do not trace the actual cause of sexual over-indulgence. Thus the problem remains unsolved.

No small achievement

Of course, there are a few people who are celibate in the full sense of the term. Sexual continence seems to be an impossible task for any human being but it can be achieved by long deliberate practice. By construction the social world is based on sex desire and therefore to root out the sex vice is no small achievement.

The inability

Even if one decides that one no longer wants to indulge in gross or subtle sex contact, one still has to deal with the powers that be and many such powers are disembodied and subtle to the extent that they are hardly traceable. The result of this is an abject failure in yoga practice, due to the inability to trace out and cancel subtle permissive sexual influences.

Monumental achievement

It is not merely a matter of distaste for sex desire or of rooting out the lusty needs, one must also face up to pressures from both embodied and disembodied entities who have predestined rights to use one's body for sexual purposes. Sexual chastity is a monumental achievement.

The most bothersome aspect

Sex desire is part and parcel of the material world and if we are to be successful we must put it aside or forget it entirely, just as children do not remember sexual habits from their former life. Adults need to make a deliberate effort to forget sex desire.

Counterproductive

Sexual pleasure is so strongly imprinted on the mind that it destroys spiritual efforts and ruins conscience. Therefore we say emphatically that it is counterproductive in the life of a yogi.

The main cause

Regulated sex pleasure or ceremonial sexual acts and spells in tantric yoga or Japanese and Chinese Tao are ultimately counterproductive because such experiments with sex pleasure cannot lead to full success in yoga, at least not in *Patañjali* ashtanga yoga. *Patañjali* lists celibacy as one of the restraints. Here is that statement:

- *Non-violence, realism, non-stealing, sexual non-expressiveness which results in the perception of spirituality (brahman) and non-possessiveness, are the moral restraints. (Yoga Sutra 2.30)*

No sexual process is satisfactory unless one intends to beget well-behaved children. We cannot overstress that the main cause of spiritual failure is sex desire.

Fight it

Understand clearly that we are not against sex itself but we oppose the use of sex for pleasure purposes only. Sex is good for generating progeny and for that matter, progeny or new bodies cannot be produced on this level without sexual indulgence. On one hand, we want people to beget progeny, to give relief to those who require bodies but on the other hand, we do not want over-indulgence merely to enjoy through the genitals. Liberation is postponed by sexual indulgence and therefore we must fight it anywhere we encounter it, even in ourselves.

That sort of celibacy

Full celibacy cannot be attained without yoga. The sexual energy is generated in the lower trunk of the body in the buttocks, groin and abdominal regions. It does not leave those areas unless it is forced to do so by certain yoga practices. It lingers there and does not move up. Therefore that sort of celibacy where no effort is made to lift it, is partial and incomplete. For dynamic celibacy one needs to practice yoga.

Sex-free Body

Pressure

Subtle body sex occurs in gross sexual activity and in dream states. While in dream states the gross body is rarely involved, in gross states the subtle body is always involved. Therefore, sex desire is definitely rooted in the subtle body, which is the body we will become conscious of at the time of death. This subtle body has certain energies or airs and one of these, called āpana, sponsors sex desire. This āpana corresponds to carbon dioxide and other heavy gases which occupy the lower part of the gross body. These heavy airs promote sexual desire and create the necessary pressure in the groin area for sexual indulgence and ongoing sexual attraction.

Techniques

Most people breathe shallowly and even prāṇāyāma yogis breathe shallowly when they are relaxed. Therefore the gross body is air-deprived and the subtle body is starved of subtle energy (prāṇā). A simple test can be made to see if your body is praṇa-starved. Sit with your spine straight and begin breathing as forcefully and rapidly as you can, in and out, in and out, as quickly as possible, blowing out and pulling in as vigorously as you can. If you notice that after a short time, your lower abdomen begins to burn, then your body is imbalanced with more polluting air than fresh air. In that case, your body is not a celibate body, since the carbon dioxide sponsors the storage and use of life energy in the groin area, thus starving the upper spine and brain. Yogis have techniques for reversing this situation. They use methods to force the polluted air up and out of the body so that the fresh air (praṇa) can go to the lower regions to keep those areas light and sex-free.

More time

The average person spends more time thinking of sex than anything else. This is evident by the prevalence of sexually-revealing and sexually-suggestive clothing.

Sexual vibrations

Men wear very tight clothing that clamps down on their bodily curves, revealing the contour of the genital and buttocks, while women do the same in very tight attire which show the contour of the breasts, the inset of the vagina and buttocks. Under the circumstances, many of us are bombarded with sexual vibrations, on nearly every association.

Victimize ourselves

The tendency to wear such sexually-revealing clothing is so strong that even persons who practice yoga and who are repeatedly told about the danger of such clothing to themselves and others, cannot give up the habit of wearing such garments. When we wear such clothing we victimize ourselves and others with our bulging penises, testes, vaginal, groin and buttocks areas. But we should not forget that the animals move unrestrictedly without clothing. Thus there is nothing special about nudity or skin-tight clothing.

More distracting

We should understand that for a human being, sexually-revealing clothing is more distracting than animal nudity. For one thing, the genitals of a male or female horse or cow are under no stress from form-fitting clothes. The human being's tight clothing squeezes the genitals. It draws the attention of the wearer and observers to the genital area.

Follows the mind

There is nothing more exhaustive than sexual intercourse. The vital energy or kundalini follows the mental focus. If we consciously or unconsciously become preoccupied with the genitals, the vital energy goes there and the brain is starved of energy.

Robs the person

A soul using a male body can readily understand that sex is exhausting. After a discharge, the male body becomes depleted of energy and a psychological darkness descends over the mind and feelings, a darkness that induces sleep and robs the person of clarity.

Exhaustion

In the case of the female body, the soul is handicapped because the body is constructed in such a way that it draws power from the male discharge of energies and this occurs on the gross as well as subtle levels. Of course nature's purpose for this is to transfer seminal fluids for the formation of new baby forms. A woman does not experience the same exhaustion a male endures from a sexual climax.

Sexual renunciation

Evidence of female exhaustion is given during the menstrual cycle when females become irritable, nervous and disagreeable, supersensitive in the emotional way. Further evidence is given when the female is pregnant and tires easily. This reveals that for males, the energy leaves the body, so the male has no illusions about exhaustion. For females, the energy is certainly discharged also but a portion is stored in the body. This storage in her body presents the illusion of added energy or enthusiasm to continue in sexual involvements.

The subtle body as well

The illusion regarding the storage is clearly dispelled when all such stored energy is discharged during menstruation and the female feels relieved after the drainage; or the relief occurs at parturition when the child is expelled from the mother's body and the woman requires weeks of rest.

We can understand this

In pregnancy the subtle body is even more involved than the earthly one. Technically speaking, a disembodied soul requiring rebirth cannot possibly enter a gross body. The soul has to enter into the subtle body of the potential parent. It enters into the feelings of the parent and from there gets into the psyche and then becomes unified with the parent's bloodstream. From there it enters into semen or ova. Therefore its actual basis of entry is the subtle body, the body of mental and emotional maneuvers. The subtle body is as much involved in sex as the gross one. We can realize this by sexual encounters in dreams.

Definitely

I cannot overstress the need for sexual restraint and again I emphasize that sex desire is the main cause for failure in yoga practice. It should not be ignored. Sex desire must definitely be brought under control.

Two chakras

There are many centers or chakras in the head area and here, we list six of them. Those who are familiar with yoga know that usually two chakras are listed; the brow center and the crown chakra, but there are others. These areas should be developed so that we replace our sexual focus with brain focus in an effort to reverse the downward trend of thoughts and feelings.

Four more

In this diagram, please note the usual brow and crown chakras. These are the main chakras listed in yoga books.

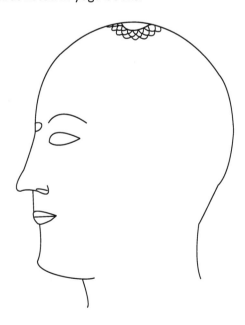

In the diagram to the right, we add four more chakras, namely the flickering *lalāta* chakra, the back top of head chakra, the medulla chakra at the base of the skull, and the ear sound chakra.

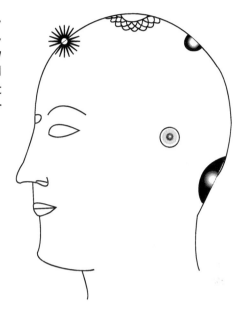

Lalāta Chakra.

The *lalāta* chakra is at the top curve of the forehead. It can be easily seen early in the morning in a dark place just after rising from bed. If one looks up to see it, it will disappear but if one keeps the eyes looking downwards in the dark, one may see it flickering with a crystal or yellow color like a flickering miner's light. This chakra may also be seen if one is in a dark room and a bright electric light is momentarily flicked on and off. In the ensuing darkness one may see this light, as the subtle body reacts to the sudden changes in the physical environment.

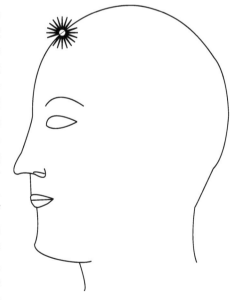

Sound Chakra

The ear sound chakra is rarely seen and it is only perceptible to yoga masters who practiced consistently and who entered the fourth dimension of awareness.

Back Top Chakra

The back top chakra is used by yogis who enter samadhi, contemplative state, in other dimensions of awareness. They take refuge there to detoxify the contaminated mind. So long as we remain attached to the forehead area in meditation it is understood that we are only beginners in the process. Brow concentration gives one more directive power in life but such direction is usually oriented to mundane achievements. When the yogi gets to the back of the brain or the back of the mind in the subtle body, he becomes freed from the struggle for existence and enters what is called the vast sky or undifferentiated clear spiritual effulgence.

Brow Chakra

For a beginner, the crown chakra simply does not exist and he cannot locate the back top chakra; but he can easily find the brow center if he has a little guidance. The brow chakra is the reference point in ordinary meditation.

Astral Existence after Death

The Recurring Instinct to Enter One's Dead Gross Body

The life

At the time of death of the gross body, one cannot re-enter that form. The privilege of awakening to this gross existence is suspended for the time being. Thus one may feel frustrated or feel as if dead, meaning that one feels that one can no longer participate in social affairs. Being unfamiliar with the subtle terrain of the hereafter, one may feel deprived of life or living ability, while in fact one is the life which is now absent from the gross body.

To awaken in a room

At the time of death one will, more than likely, try to re-enter the gross body repeatedly but unsuccessfully. While the body lives, the soul repeatedly re-enters from dream states. It becomes accustomed to this and takes this for granted. When the gross body dies, one finds that this ability to re-enter is suspended or one may feel that the ability to awaken in a room in the home was suddenly cancelled. That realization may be shocking.

Wake up as a physical body

Yet, one will repeatedly try and repeatedly become frustrated. What is that repeated effort to enter the body? It is merely the desire to wake up as a physical body. It is a mental act; the same mental instinct which one used throughout the life of the body. It is the act of waking up. After the death of the gross form, one finds that such a mental act only results in one remaining in the dream state. This causes confusion, disappointment and depression. The next action is to consult with relatives and friends, trying to get them to awaken the dead earthly form. Or one may try to get them to acknowledge one's existence without realizing that they cannot perceive the subtle dream body. One may become ignorant of one's subtle condition and feel that the subtle body is the gross one, while in fact it merely feels like the earthly one which is dead. One may try to talk to relatives and friends, to touch them and become familiar as before, only to discover that they don't respond, because they focused on gross existence only and are insensitive to the subtle dream world.

Acknowledge one's existence

Feeling frustrated, one will repeatedly try to reach them during the night when their gross bodies are asleep and their subtle forms are free and active in the dream world. One will try to get them to acknowledge one's existence but they will deny it, telling one that one is supposed to be dead. They will be fearful, feeling one is a ghost, or a bad memory.

Entering the bodies of relatives

After some days, when the dead gross body begins to decay or after it is cremated, one will be unable to find that body and thus the efforts to enter it will cease. At that time one will begin entering the body of relatives and friends, trying to eat through their mouths or handle physical objects through their hands and perform other activities through them. One's friends and relatives may change habits just to suit one but they may do so unconsciously without even realizing that they were influenced by one's view.

Haunt or inhabit the room

Another activity of such a departed soul is to haunt or inhabit the room where the previous body used to retire. One may remain there for up to forty days after death, and in some cases one may remain there for years. One may do so in the subtle form. One's presence may be felt by others, who feel spooked while in that area. A sensitive person may be possessed of sleeplessness or may be fearful of sleeping while in that room.

Tool of action

After forty days one may realize that one is dead. One may not be perceptive enough to realize that if one can think of one's death, one is certainly not dead but only dead in the sense that one was deprived of one's tool of action in the earthly world; that tool of action being the previous flesh body. One may think to oneself, "I am dead. Something happened. I cannot act as I used to. I am a ghost."

Their response

At that point one may again try to consult with relatives and friends who possess living earthly forms. One may influence any of them to complete unfinished obligations. One will perceive that they can sense one's thinking but their response may be indifferent or negative, and therefore one may feel disqualified or powerless.

Master oneself

If one realizes how one leaves and re-enters the gross body nightly during sleep or rest, one can better master oneself in the hereafter and avoid days, weeks or months of mental confusion.

Chapter 4

Third eye Grasp

The third eye or brow chakra is one of the standard points of reference for yogis. Indeed that point is such an ancient reference that it is mentioned in the Bhagavad Gītā.

- *Excluding the external sensual contacts, and fixing the visual focus between the eyebrows, putting the inhalation and exhalation in balance, moving through the nose...*
- *...the wise man, who is dedicated to achieving liberation, whose sensual energy, mind and intellect are controlled, whose desire, fear and anger are gone, is liberated always. (Bhagavad Gītā 5.27-28)*
- *...and that meditator who even at the time of death, with an unwavering mind, being connected devotedly, with psychological power developed through yoga practice, and having caused the energizing breath to enter between the eyebrows with precision, goes to the Divine Supreme Person. (Bhagavad Gītā 8.10)*

If one passes from the body before reaching an advanced stage, one who mastered the third eye focus may use it to keep the mind from taking shelter in false hopes. Krishna guaranteed that one who at the time of death, fixes the life air as well as the attention between the eyebrows, and in full devotion engages with full attention remembering Krishna, not being distracted by anything, will certainly attain the Divine Supreme Person. The technical Sanskrit terms *prāṇāpānau* and *prāṇam āveśya* indicate that the person gained control of the life force and is a complete celibate. Celibacy is part of this particular course. *Yoga balena* indicates complete conservation of one's spiritual energies to the extent of not being distracted by celestial beauties. If one is not completely celibate he will certainly be distracted, no matter what, and he will not reach the spiritual places, even though he will remain as an exceptional person.

After getting some grasp on the third eye, one reaches a stage of being able to handle that chakra so as to bring it into focus as desired. This is necessary in the advanced stages of the practice. At the time of death one may not have time to wait patiently for the mind to settle down, the life force to be pulled up, and the chakra to become visible or perceptible. Therefore after days, weeks or years as the case may be, after one masters this chakra, one no longer waits for it to settle down but settles it down forcibly by a practice of grasping.

This chakra can be grasped if one knows its location and whereabouts and if one knows how it is manifested and how it goes out of manifestation due to confusion, anxiety, or distraction.

In grasping this chakra one uses the attention and will power. One uses the attention as if it were mental fingers or clasping instruments.

The clarity achieved by the ancient yogis at this chakra is impossible today except for short periods of time. Therefore one has to learn the grasping method and the clearing method of removing the mental fog that clouds the clear space of this chakra. One must also learn to move the revolving, rotating disc energy of this chakra, closer to one's central position in the psychic center of the brain. Here are diagrams which explain this information in a visual way.

The core-self is located at the psychic center of the brain space.

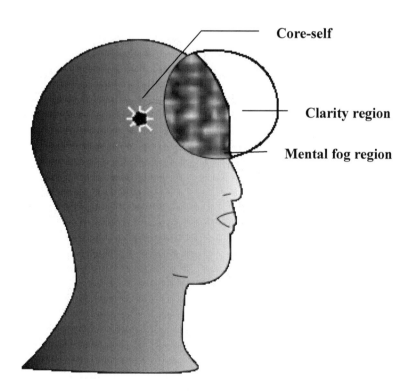

Core-self

Clarity region

Mental fog region

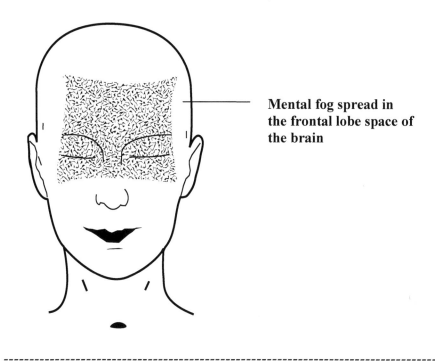

Mental fog spread in
the frontal lobe space of
the brain

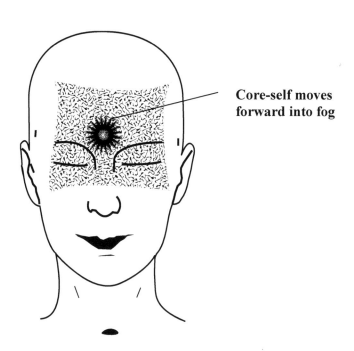

Core-self moves
forward into fog

Core-self in mental fog

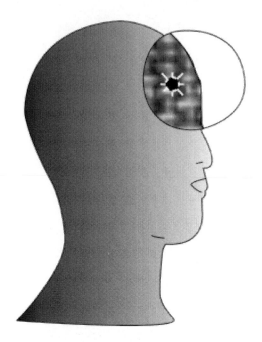

Core-self in clarity outside the skull area

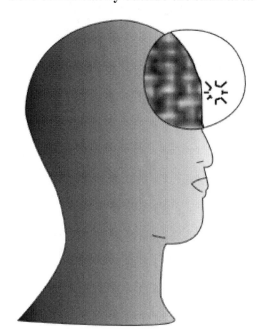

Core-self pushing mental fog to back of brain

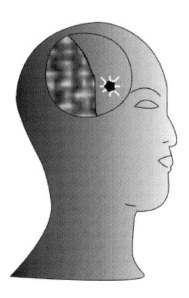

Mental fog dissipated, while the core-self remains in back of brain

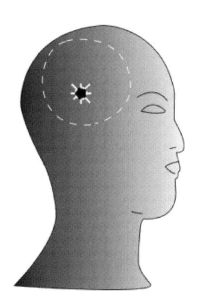

Fog cannot exist in back portion of brain since the calculative power that creates and supports fog is non-existent there. When fog is taken there it clears away like a morning mist dissipating naturally.

Chapter 5

Third-eye Clarity Peering

In these diagrams, the core-self remains at the psychic center of the brain and looks through clear spaces which appear suddenly at the brow chakra.

Continue focusing between the eyebrows even if you do not see anything there. In time, you will develop astral vision.

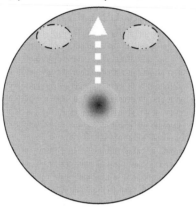

Star speck seen at brow chakra

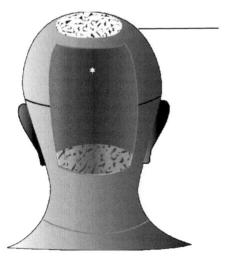

Crown of head

Tear-shaped clear space at 3rd eye

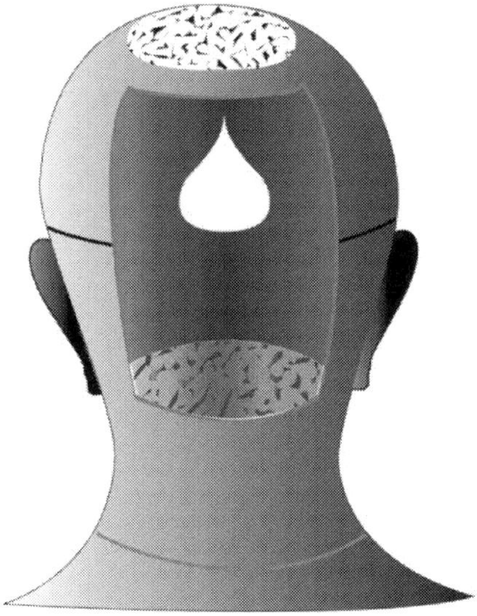

Oval shape at 3rd eye

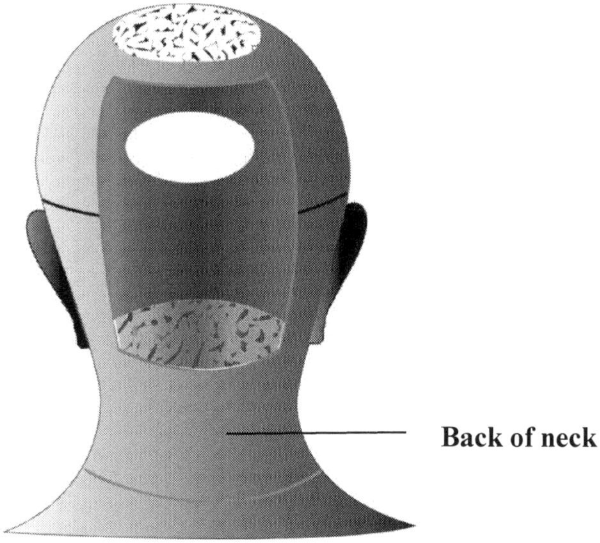

Square shape at 3rd eye

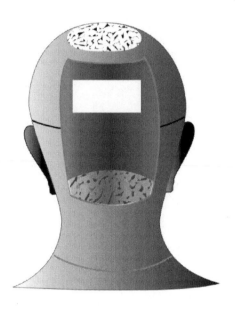

Eight-pointed star shape opening at 3rd eye

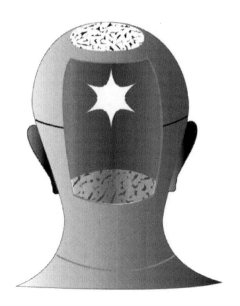

Natural scene appearing through square opening at 3rd eye

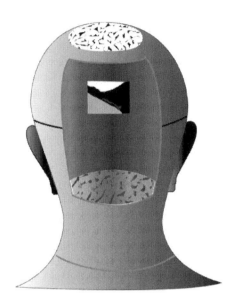

Clarity Soul Peering

In meditation one may perceive a mystic cloud of dark mental and emotional energy. The core-self identifies with this energy.

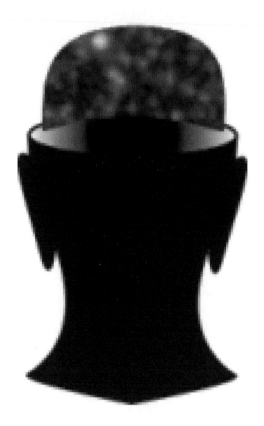

Back of head

The diagram below shows two layers of confusion and absorption mental energy with a neutral gap between. The core-self is perplexed by this energy and is aware of itself as a spatial object of consciousness, with its energy travelling outwards in all directions.

In the diagram below the core-self is free from the dominance of dark mental energy, feeling itself as a localized spatial force.

Chapter 6

Thought Identification

According to *Patañjali*, yoga begins with restrained thought patterns. *Patañjali*, an authority on the methods of classical yoga, says that the cessation of mental constructions is the accomplishment of yoga.

The mind switches

The ideas of the mind are natural because the mind is fickle, moving restlessly from one view to another. By nature the mind cannot settle down unless it is filled with a mass of dulling energies. As long as the mind is energized even in a minor way, it begins modifications or changes. In meditation this is the first thing a person observes, that the mind switches from one idea to another, from one thought or scene to another, from taking information from one sense to another, continuously and impulsively. This action of the mind is of course against the stability of the self. It dissipates the energy of the self inefficiently and purposelessly.

Tracing Foreign Thoughts

One needs to develop a method of tracing foreign thoughts which enter the mind. One should identify particular persons who are sources of such mental constructions.

Methods of identifying sources of foreign thoughts:

- recording thoughts
- checking conversations and correspondence to find matches for thoughts
- checking associations and emotional transfers to find motivations which produce desirable and undesirable thoughts

In the beginning, the identification of foreign thoughts is hardly possible since one usually assumes that all thoughts are one's ideas. This confusion regarding thoughts occurs because of an ill-defined sense of identity in trying to take possession of everything within the psyche. However, as one strives to come to grips with the mind's whimsical thinking ability, one soon begins to realize that certain thoughts have to be foreign, since one finds that one has no deep interest in many of the ideas and visions that occur in the mind.

Notations are beneficial

At this stage one should decide to trace thoughts. This tracing may begin with writing down disturbing or spiritually non-productive ideas. One who has good memory may avoid the written process and just take mental note of such thoughts, but still the writer feels that notations are beneficial, since even if one has a good memory, the experience of a foreign thought is apt to sink to the subconscious level.

Identify that source

After the thought is noted one has to wait for an indication of its source. For instance, if one receives phone calls or letters and any of these discusses a certain foreign thought, one can then identify that source.

System of thought tracking

If, for instance, one has another such thought, and then meets an acquaintance who immediately begins discussing the subject of the thought without one's mentioning it, then one can again identify that person as the source. Thus one can develop a system of thought tracking.

The source

Once one begins to recognize the pattern of another's thoughts or ideas, it becomes easy to know when a particular thought originated in another person's psyche and not in one's own. That is the first step in obtaining freedom from foreign ideas. Perhaps one reaches a point of losing interest in sexual indulgence and then one has a sex thought. One may conclude that this thought is coming from another person. Thus one should not act out the sexual impulse but should patiently wait to see if anyone can be identified as the source of the sexual idea. For instance, suppose after having a sexual thought, one reaches a friend who immediately begins speaking about sexual affairs. One could identify that friend as the source. Or suppose instead one reaches someone who is sexually attracted to oneself and suppose that person makes a sexual remark, romantic speech or flirtation; then one can identify the person as the source.

Subject to outside influence

In this way one can realize in all honesty that one's mind is sensitive to the desire of others. One's mind is not isolated. One's mind is subject to outside influences. One's mind is automatically open to thought energies from others.

Thought Stoppage
Mental energy

Thought stoppage is an item on the list of things to achieve in spiritual life because thinking energy, subtle energy, is valuable power. In the conditioned state we do not realize the value of this energy. In fact, in the neophyte stage all transcendentalists fail to realize the importance of regulating thinking activity. This is due to ignorance about the value of mental force. In conditioned life, one values worldly goods and is careless about the usage of mental and emotional energies. Mental energy is more important than money or any commodity that money can buy.

Thoughts cost energy

Advanced yoga uses thought stoppage as its foundation. Thoughts cost energy. Spiritually nonproductive thoughts waste psychological energy. Thoughts that originate in the minds of relatives, friends, enemies, casual acquaintances, and even in the minds of fellow seekers and which are spiritually-nonproductive, do waste valuable power. Such thoughts weaken us spiritually. They reduce spiritual advancement.

Identification of the source of a foreign thought is an important accomplishment. The next step is to find a way to rid oneself of such thoughts before they bring one to a lower level.

In the beginning when one recognizes these thoughts, the recognition occurs after one was affected, but that is not satisfactory. Take, for example, my friend who thought of getting a girlfriend for sexual purposes. His thought was transferred to my mind. Then I felt a need to have a sexual contact. Later I realize that this person was the source of the idea. In the meantime I engaged in a sexual indulgence. Therefore even though I later identified him as the source, I was affected and was implicated.

Enters my mind

Take, for example, my friend who had unreasonable, impractical ideas of life. He had these because of misconceptions about reality. He suffered through life with these. If he had an impractical idea and if it entered my mind and I tried to live it out, I would have acted carelessly due to ignorance. I may realize that he is the source, but I will suffer nevertheless.

Recognizing the source

It is essential that we master the art of recognizing the source of foreign thoughts as the thoughts appear and not long after. That is the only way to nullify any impulse that arises as a result of a foreign idea.

Always susceptible

The secret to curbing foreign thoughts is to be non-responsive to incoming thoughts. A very sensitive radio detects sound vibrations automatically even from a great distance. It processes these vibrations, passes a signal through an amplifier and through a speaker and then we hear the reproduced sound. The sound does not originate in the radio. Similarly many ideas, thoughts, and pictures within the mind originate elsewhere and travel through space to reach the sensitive mind. A radio can be turned off but the mind is not turned off as easily; it is always energized. The mind is always susceptible to thoughts and signals from others.

No response

Initially when a thought enters the mind, one should not respond to it. If one senses the source of the thought one should immediately consider whether or not to respond. If one entertains a thought, further impulses are generated in the mind and one may then act impulsively.

Easier

Getting rid of thoughts that belong to people we do not like is easier than getting rid of spiritually non-productive thoughts of friends and fellow seekers.

A non-responsive attitude

In the higher dimensions, one does not have to worry about spiritually destructive thoughts. Those planes are out of the range of lowly ideas; just as a high frequency radio would not pick up low frequency transmissions. Persons in the higher dimensions are not plagued with lowly thoughts, but we can resist them by a non-responsive attitude. As long as we are on this level we should deal with trashy thoughts by giving no response to them.

Mentally separated

The technique is to disregard each spiritually-destructive idea as soon as it is realized by the mind. One should remain mentally separated from the idea and starve it of attention. Then it will be powerless.

The tiniest bit of energy

Many thoughts from external sources form a question in the mind. Such question-energy requires a response in the form of a mental answer, comment, opinion, or reply. As soon as one envisions such thoughts, one must stop the mind from responding. One has to give up the tendency for involvement even within the mind and let such thoughts exist without investing the tiniest bit of energy in them.

Necessary

We must realize that these austerities are necessary if we want to reach the super-consciousness.

Dream Clarity

Dream clarity is no small achievement. It is essential to our effort at self-realization. For one thing, if we do not have clarity in the dream world, in dream encounters, if we are lacking in discrimination and crisp awareness of that level, we will also lack clarity at the time of death.

To believe that one's confusion in dreams or one's lack of dream recall is not related to the confusion one will face in the hereafter, is a fool's faith only.

Examining the Physical Body at Night

Insensitivity

Remembrance of dreams is directly related to the intensity of the dreams and to the energized state of the material body. By intensity of dreams, I mean the ghastliness or desirability of the dream. Many people are only aware of their nightmares or ghastly dreams which literally brand their minds with a frightening impression. For instance, during the teen years of this present body, I viewed movies. On some occasions I saw horror films. After seeing such films I had terrible dreams based on the horror images. At the same time other dream activity that left only a slight impression on the mind, may not be remembered. These dreams of slight impression are also important but may not be recalled due to the insensitivity of consciousness to the dream world.

Very mild impression

Later on, however, when I began to make spiritual progress and to shed the association of childhood, I remembered even the subtle dreams of very mild impression.

No memory of astral life

Another important factor in dream recall is the energized or fatigued condition of the material body. If the material body is not energized in the late afternoon or early evening or some other time just before resting, one will hardly remember dreams. One might falsely conclude that there are no astral encounters. Just as the materialistic person feels that there was no past life because he has no memory of it, one might feel that there are no dreams because one has no memory of astral life.

Dream clarity

The importance of dream clarity is its ability to make us conscious of ourselves on the astral level so that we are not stupefied on that plane. For instance, a renunciant who took a vow of celibacy can guard himself in the waking hours of the day, but unless he has crisp awareness during dreams, he cannot guard himself in that dimension. He may in stupor engage his subtle body in sexual intercourse on that plane. Technically speaking, that would be a violation of vows, which may lead to sexual contact on the physical plane.

The expense

At night the physical body sleeps but it also draws energy from the subtle one. If it has to digest food due to late eating, it must draw more energy from the subtle body to complete that activity. Any operations of blood renewal, cell renewal, digestion, evacuation, storage of urine and storage of feces, any or all of these activities at night, are done at the expense of the subtle body.

Less dream recall

Therefore these activities should be reduced to the greatest extent so that the subtle body can be more energized; the more energy it gives to the gross one, the less dream recall there will be.

Increased dream awareness

If at all possible, one should do rapid breathing to pump additional oxygen into the gross body before sleeping. This extra oxygen would be stored in the blood cells, and the gross body will then require less energy from the subtle one. Thus the subtle one will have increased dream awareness.

Separates from the gross body

When the subtle body separates from the gross body during sleep, it is a connected separation. At death there is a psychic disconnection. During sleep the separated bodies are connected. There is a continuous transfer of energy between the two forms. If the subtle body has to transfer too much energy to the gross one, the subtle form is drained considerably and the entity will function in an unconscious stupor in the astral world. In some cases one separates from the gross body and goes to a distant place and in other cases one remains in the subtle body in near proximity to the gross one. In either condition, the recall of dreams is directly proportionate to the energy conservation of the subtle body. Regular dream recall is possible for a person whose subtle body gives little energy to the sleeping gross form.

Some aids to dream recall are:

- ✓ *total darkness*
- ✓ *lack of noise*
- ✓ *lack of electrical noise from appliances and machinery*
- ✓ *lack of stress*
- ✓ *early meals*
- ✓ *moderate quantities of food*
- ✓ *sexual continence*

Total darkness helps with dream recall since the brain of the physical body is stimulated by light vibrations. It is a proven fact that the pineal and pituitary glands are affected by light sensation. The pineal gland is directly affected by light or darkness and the pituitary is affected by sensual assessments.

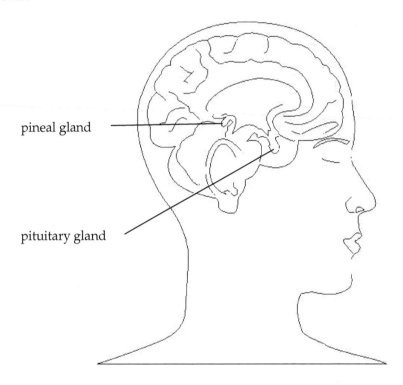

pineal gland

pituitary gland

Location of Glands

Sunlight

If for instance one tries to sleep in the presence of full sunlight in an open field, it may take more time to fall asleep. Rest would be assumed quicker under a shade tree. Sunlight and even electrical lights startle the brain. In fact, sunlight penetrates the skull and activates the brain.

Less energy

Total darkness is conducive to dream recall since by it the physical brain moves into a mode of minimal activity, thus taking less energy from the subtle one for its maintenance. Those who are afraid of the dark or who must sleep with lights, can take advantage by covering their forehead with a dark cotton cloth so that the lights do not penetrate through the cloth into the skull to disturb the brain.

Dream recall

Dead silence is preferred around a sleeping body for full dream recall. Sexual continence or celibacy is also required, for when males pass semen or alternately when females pass vaginal liquids in intercourse, either party tires out the subtle body and the gross one, making dream recall difficult. Late eating is counterproductive of dream recall because the digestive activity in the stomach pulls much energy from the subtle form.

The Life Force as the Subconscious

Layers and layers

In modern psychology the subconscious is recognized as the section of the mind which holds forgotten impressions of the past. Most Westerners feel that it holds impressions from one's childhood only and not from any time prior to that. However, the subconscious is a real compartment of the psyche. It holds the impressions of all past lives compressed within it in a storage form in layers and layers of psychological impressions.

Location

The subconscious and conscious minds are regarded as two parts of one mind. First of all, it is a matter of location in the subtle body. Subsequently it is also a matter of location in the gross body. The average human being cannot sort the different parts of the psyche. He or she feels that the physical body, subtle body, mentality, and decisive self are one principle only.

Separated

The subconscious is not prominent in the head. It comes into the head during split-second flashes of enlightenment, when the life force is energized. The core-self is separate from it. The I-self rarely reaches the memories of past lives which are stored on the subconscious level.

Follows the generative energy

As soon as one gets serious about celibacy and as soon as one finds a master of celibacy to give the method of its practice, one begins to understand that unless one ceases sexual flirtation and connections, one cannot make advancement. This is because the life force cannot be freed from the lower part of the body unless sexual indulgence is stopped entirely. The life force follows the generative energy in the subtle and gross bodies. Unless the generative energy is purified to the extent that it no longer has a lusty flavor, one cannot free the life force and it will remain in a lusty state, being interested in generating progeny, having sexual indulgence and passing from the gross body with residual sexual concerns.

Reformed

Yogis who realize this problem with the life force undertake elaborate austerities to purify it, since one cannot be liberated entirely unless the life force is reformed.

Chapter 7

The Continuous Naad Sound

There is at all times in all places, a continuous Naad sound. This sound is mentioned in the Uddhava Gītā.

- *In the heart chakra, the Om sound which is like the continuous peal of a bell, resonates continually, like a fibre in a lotus stalk. Raising it by using the vitalizing energy, one should blend that sound with the musical tones. (Uddhava Gītā 9.34)*

- *By continuous linking of his attention with the concentration force which is focused on subtle sound within the mind, and on Me in the spiritual atmosphere and in the energizing energy, the advanced yogin directly hears the sounds of distant living beings. (Uddhava Gītā 10.19)*

- *In performing full purification within his body, by air and by fire, he should meditate on the effortless linking of his attention to the concentration force which connects with My subtle but supreme partial manifestation, which is situated on a lotus in the bosom area, and which the perfected yogis experience at the end of their progression through naad subtle sound resonation. (Uddhava Gītā 22.23)*

If one sits by the ocean there is a constant roaring, as wave after wave comes in. If one remains quiet within the mind space, after the senses are withdrawn from external interest, one will find that there is a constant sound within the being. This is the Naad or Nada sound. Yogis are particularly interested in this sound as it is perpetually expressed within and can be heard clearly and distinctly. It relieves one for the need of a mantra, so that one can focus within the psyche without props.

Sound

The sky or atmospheric space is the first dimension developed in the universe and the corresponding quality of sound developed thereafter. Sound is essential. In the beginning one will not see into the spiritual world visually. One will not touch persons in the spiritual world, or taste spiritual foods, or smell spiritual odors.

Flushes the mind

First one hears this sound on the inner side of the right ear. It is heard as a continuous blend of high-pitched frequencies. It is continuous without interruption and only if one breaks away from it by giving one's attention to the subtle or gross world, does one lose perception of it. This sound flushes the mind of random ideas, worries, troubles, and lower associations of all sorts.

A high-pitched frequency

If one reaches a quiet place and then presses the lower and upper right jaws together, one's focus will shift to the right side of the head and one may hear a high-pitched frequency for as long as one can apply the pressure. As soon as the pressure is eased and the jaw is relaxed, one may still hear this tone.

Relief from anxiety

Once one learns to put the mind on this sound, one can find it any time during the day or night. One should meditate on it and get relief from anxiety. This sound also occurs on the inner side of the left ear but its frequency there is slightly different. However, as soon as one reaches this sound, he will find that his mind repeatedly tries to return to mundane thoughts and gross objects. Thus one might be drawn away from the listening practice to become involved in mundane affairs.

At that inner point

By careful study one can begin to understand that the spontaneous melody coming from the inner right ear, comes into the ear with a pulling vibration as if to pull the spark-like thinker through that sound into the spiritual environment while the sound entering the left ear has a slightly different melody and comes through the inner ear with a pushing vibration as if to hold the attention of the listener at that inner point.

A complex melody

If one listens to the right side, then to the left, then to the right, then to the left again, the sounds blend into a complex melody that fills the entire head. The sounds produced may twinkle melodiously into one blend.

Contamination

Mind-speech

In listening to this internal continuous sound, one realizes how one is constantly hunted down and disturbed by foreign thoughts. For instance, these thoughts do not reach the extreme right side of the brain but they reach the central brain area and they are slightly left of center. These thoughts reach that zone and the mind forcibly responds with mind-speech.

Automatically re-transmitted

How does one associate with foreign thoughts that penetrate the mind? One does so by responding mentally wherein one perceives a question or conceives of an image and responds to the energy within the mind. These responses are then automatically re-transmitted to the person whose thought penetrated the mind.

The cessation of thought patterns

These thoughts grasp one and pull one away from the divine sound. In the advanced state of meditation, one no longer creates impulsive or reactive thoughts patterns, but one is still harassed and hunted down by the thought patterns. It is with this consideration that *Patañjali* began the *Yoga Sūtras* by stating that he would begin a discourse on yoga which is the cessation of thought patterns, ideas and visualizations.

Pull away

When I asked the Acharya Gambhiranatha if particular foreign thoughts were ever banished by the ancient yogis, he replied, "They certainly were." He stated further, "In the beginning of the thought control, which is described in detail in the *Patañjali Yoga Sūtras*, we controlled the mind rigidly by *pratyāhāra* sensual retraction, which is internalizing and isolating the senses from their objects. But we found that unless one is very serious he cannot complete this stage. It is not just a matter of determination either. It relies on whether one can pull away from the material world and not regret the resulting isolation.

Would not regress

"If a student advances and begins to live pleasantly in the isolation, he reaches the first stage of *dhyāna*, which is freedom from the thinking and conceiving mind. To reach this stage is a joy to any student and also to his teacher since if the disciple attains this, it is a sure signal that he will not regress.

First stage of happiness

"Once this first stage is mastered in terms of controlling the impulsive thoughts, one reaches the first stage of happiness and that is described in the Gītā as the stage of finding joy in one's nature.

> • *Indeed, being psychologically pacified, the yogi, whose emotions are calmed, who is on the spiritual plane, who is free from bad tendencies, experiences superior happiness. (Bhagavad Gītā 6.27)*

Outside their psychic range

"However, soon after one reaches this stage, he finds that there is another problem in the form of foreign thoughts which seek one out. As soon as one is accomplished in the art of checking whimsical and impulsive thoughts, friends and enemies take relief from the curtailment of thought projection which used to emanate from one's mind. They experience this subconsciously. They feel happiness because one no longer places mental demands on them. In that happiness they stop sending thought patterns for a time. However, later on, they begin to feel that one is outside their psychic range."

Stop associative thoughts

At this point the author interjected and asked the yogi, "O master of the yoga process, explain to us how one can get beyond this stage. One has little or no control over the thoughts of others, or over their spiritual development. How is it possible for us to stop associative thoughts? Explain the method used by ancient ascetics to achieve this."

Location of Foreign Thoughts

Not budge an inch

Mahāyogin Gambhiranatha replied, "It is very simply done. At first one cannot help but run internally to such thoughts. As soon as one runs to the part of the mind where the thought occurs, one should not touch or respond to the energy. One becomes conscious of the internal landscape, just as one would run physically to assist a friend who requests assistance. One actually moves from one place within the mind to another place where the thought occurred. Initially one cannot stop this running process but one should not react to the thought in any case. That is the first stage. As soon as one masters this, one moves to the next stage which is to remain with the divine sound internally and not budge an inch to reach any thought, idea or visualization which forms in the mind.

The real solution

"If one is tired, if the subtle body is not properly surcharged with oxygenized energy, you will find that you cannot remain with the divine sound. You will find that you must go to the place of thought reception. In that case, one should trick the mind by retreating from the internal level just a little and being slightly external and then the thoughts will go away. This is similar to the habit of awaking from a bad dream. If one has a bad dream, one tries to wake up on this side of existence to avoid it. It is a similar experience. But this method of escaping from the internal plane is not the real solution. The real solution is to remain with the divine sound, to enter into it."

Electrical center of the brain

Thoughts which come from agreeable acquaintances come to the electrical center of the brain. Those which are from dear acquaintants who are troublesome come from a place slightly left of the electrical center and those which come from others and which require some intellectual analysis come from a position further left from the center.

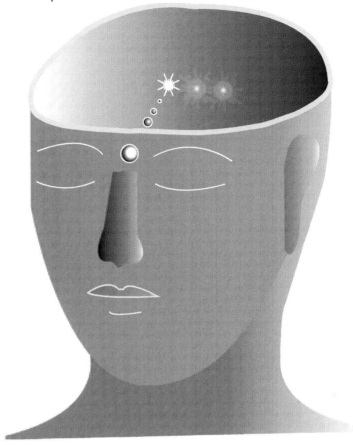

Using a Non-forceful Method of Pulling the Life Force into the Brain
Cannot remain elevated

Yogiraj Gambhiranatha showed me a method used by some yogis to lift the life force into the brain without using the *prāṇāyāma* techniques. He said that in most cases yogis who excel at this method are persons who performed *prāṇāyāma* previously and who purified the gross and subtle bodies through it. According to his view, a person whose body is not purified can use this method but he will do so unsuccessfully since the life force will not remain in the brain but will descend to the base. It cannot remain elevated in a contaminated body.

A pathway

After being firmly established in the divine sound, hearing it internally, and after doing this for months, a yogi changes in nature and becomes calm, dispassionate and non-violent. At that stage the yogi remains in the divine sound and directs his attention to the life force in the lower parts of the body, in the lower spinal centers. The sound current then uses the attention of the yogi as a pathway and goes down into the lower parts of the body to purify it. At that time the life force becomes attracted to it and rises up to meet the attention energy in the head.

Stability

I questioned Yogi Gambhiranatha, "Why is it that we cannot bypass the *prāṇāyāma* process?

He replied, "Stability in the ringing of the divine sound within cannot be attained by a person who is not purified. A person with a contaminated nature, may hear the sound intermittently, but he cannot listen to it consistently. In fact, he often forgets to listen for it. Thus he never achieves it continuously. He might hear from an authority who has firm faith in it but he himself cannot rely on it because he is too attached to the external situation.

Train the mind

"The accomplishment might sound easy but it takes much time for practice. First one must train the mind to hear, to accept, and to focus on it or at least to assume a passive mood so that one can focus on it.

The self and the mind

"In fact, one must realize that the mind is more attached to itself than to the person who uses it. Thus in the final analysis there will be a power struggle between the self and the mind. The mind is attached to its creative imaginary powers and the related stimuli and even if one becomes detached from these and from the mind's usefulness, still one has to struggle with the mind itself which impulsively expresses the unwanted habits and tendencies.

Clearly distinguish

"Most of all one must clearly distinguish between the self as the controller in the head, the mind as the spatial energy in the head, and the life force as the power at the base of the spine. Unless one is clear about these objects he cannot be free to focus on the divine sound within for he will be repeatedly distracted."

The Life Force is Different from the Soul

Life force units are bestowed to every individual who becomes manifest physically. The life force is definitely not the spirit itself, but without it, a spirit cannot participate in material existence.

Years ago, in 1972, I beamed up in a purified astral body to the sun planet. I experienced life there as the sun inhabitants do. This was done by a process of projected beaming of a sunlight astral body, or a bodily form created from sun energy. It is possible.

Chapter 8

Dreams

The ordinary way of identifying the subtle landscape is found in the recollection of dreams. Even the most materially-occupied person is occasionally conscious of dream states, but he or she may not believe that the experiences are real. Some Western psychologists determine dreams to be brain activity only. They say that dreams are merely a plane of impressions which are recorded during waking hours and which are triggered as fantasy during sleep. According to these experts, the brain has electric waves which produce dream images.

In the yogic view, sleep is a state in which the subtle body separates from the gross one. We are all familiar with the gross flesh-and-bones form. And the subtle one, which eludes our gross senses, is comprised of conscious mental power, emotional energies and imaginative ability. A skeptic may inquire as to why most of us do not recall such a drastic action as the separation of these bodies. In response, such an unconscious phenomena occurs due to the innate design of these bodies, which prevents us from naturally experiencing their separation from one another. The separation does occur but it is such a subtle process that one cannot observe it unless one has mystic vision and is capable of remembering the subtlest, most instantaneous occurrences.

Mystic practice may begin from having lucid dreams. By recalling all or some dreams, it is possible to gradually cultivate mystic perception. Some individuals are naturally gifted with recall power and some are not. All can achieve some degree of dream recall by practice. From the physical level we tend to minimize the importance of the subtle reality. At the time of death, however, when the gross body quits, the gross senses become obsolete and the subtle level becomes all important since at that time we relinquish the physical and function through the subtle body of mind and emotions alone.

The world of dreams is the world of the hereafter and if we could master it now, if we could chart it at this time, we would not be lost in the transition at death. To recall dreams more clearly and precisely and to be more rationally-inclined in the dream world, one may practice a particular meditation just before resting at night. This is the last mental activity one would perform before losing waking consciousness. If there are other practices such as saying prayers, chanting or any other disciplines, one should do these first and lastly one would try to pull the power from the bodily senses, especially from the visual sense. As one tries to does this, one will feel as if the power is going outward through the eyes.

Energy retrieval and drainage through eyes

The drainage through the eyes can be reversed by pulling inwards mentally. One will feel that the power is being drained backwards into the central thinker.

At a certain point when pulling in the power, one will feel that it is stabilized in the inward direction and is no longer draining outwards.

Stabilization of inward drainage

Shift energy to chest region

One should direct it towards the central chest.

This meditation may also be done in the following alternate postures.

With Knees Raised

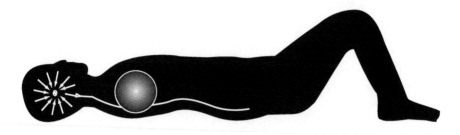

With Neck Cocked Back

With knees raised and neck cocked back

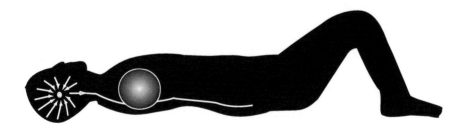

The Physical Anatomy of Spinal Nerves

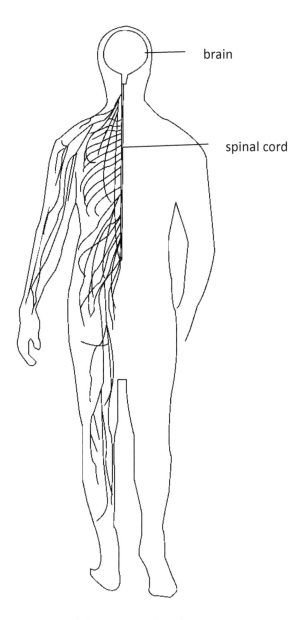

In the astral body the subtle energy distribution corresponds to the spinal cord and nerve system. This subtle distribution uses energy gyrating centers and tube-like channels. These are chakras and nadis.

When a meditator attempts to retrieve energy from the body and bring it into the core-self, he can draw the energy up from the toes, legs, fingers, arms, trunk and chest, and channel it into the spinal column through the nerves. From there the energy moves up the spine and is then transferred to the brain for control by the meditator.

As for retrieving the energy from the eyes, nose, mouth, ears, face and brain, one mentally pulls the electrical and mental energy from all areas towards the core-self.

It is essential to realize that the gross and subtle bodies are interlocked, occupying the same space whenever the gross body is awake, even though they are displaced from one another when the conscious mind does not function through the gross body.

The meditation technique described brings on sleep of the gross body and slows down the anxiety of the life force. Even in the life of a yogi there are times when the mind keeps racing when sleep is required, and the life force keeps sending energy into the mind and senses, activating them on and on. Thus one can use this technique to quiet the life force. Once it is quieted, the gross body will enter into its sleepy state automatically and one can separate from it to the subtle plane.

Expert yogis are able to consciously shift from this level to the subtle but a beginner should not be concerned with that achievement. His aim should be to become conscious in the subtle plane after he is shifted over to that side of existence. In other words, he should aim at remembering dreams, at analyzing them during the night and at become less impulsive and less sensually-oriented so that the decisions he makes in dreams are consistent with his moral and philosophical aims.

The subtle body, the dream utility, is impulsive, sensually-oriented and devoid of a sense for discrimination. The human body anchors the subtle one and may restrict its impulsive actions.

The Sleeping Impulse

All energies in the material creation have proper usage, even the negative or dulling ones. There is the mode which fosters clarity, the mode which promotes passion and the mode which spreads confusion and depression. The depressing power reduces alertness and promotes sleep. The passionate one motivates activity. The clarifying energy makes us sober, perceptive and considerate.

In yoga practice one tries his best to get far away from the depressive powers. However we cannot get rid of these energies completely. They are composites of the material world. So long as one is on the material side, even on the subtle material side which is experienced in dream states, one must by necessity deal with the dulling and passionate energies. The effort therefore is to curb one's impulsive addiction to these energies and to greatly restrict one's association with them, to minimize and reduce that as much as is permissible by reality.

As far as sleep or dullness is concerned, the material body cannot be rejuvenated on a daily basis without it. It is simply impossible because that is the nature of the body. The substances of the body such as solids, liquids, gases and spaces are all material elements which by nature are in the mode of ignorance, the dulling mode. Therefore one cannot at any stage turn the material body into a spiritual reality. One can use the body for spiritual realization but the body itself by constitution is rooted in material nature. The teacher is animated but his chalk is not. Therefore he animates the chalk. Still even though it is animated and is put to use by the intelligent teacher, it remains a substance without life. In the same way the substances which comprise the material body are animated by spiritual and psychic powers, but the body retains its material composition.

Thus the ideal effort is to use the body for divine purposes and keep it as healthy and fit as is permissible. Since the body requires sleep, one should regulate sleep rather than deprive the body of it. A yogi should put the gross body to rest while he simultaneously keeps the mind alert and the spirit active on other levels of existence.

The reduction of the dulling influence over the gross body is a task for us. We must also achieve the reduction of this dulling influence over the subtle body and life force. If we do not achieve this, we will have to continue in our present condition with these influences expressing themselves haphazardly through us and against our will.

The dulling forces of the body and mind are increased by bad association. The beginning point of curbing this is to understand bad association. We can notice that when we are with certain people, we experience an increase of enthusiasm or a decrease of it accordingly and from that understanding we can begin to curb undesirable association. It is simply a matter of observation. So much of spiritual life has to do with observing, considering and deciding to go ahead with or to cease some type of association that appears to be or not to be in our spiritual interest.

Essentially spiritual life necessitates great reductions in association since most associations are conducive to mundane expression without spiritual understanding.

Social involvement with lower entities, even lower human beings, produces an increase in the dulling forces that operate in the psyche. When the physical body becomes tired, it drains energy from the subtle one during sleep. This drainage of energy shuts down the recall power of dreams. No recall means that there was dream activity but the subtle form was too drained to permit memory.

In advanced practice, one's required morality or social behavior applies to dream states. A violation on the dream level is a deviation as well. Therefore we cannot afford to be unconscious on the subtle level. We must be conscious there so that we can maintain our principles even on that plane.

Habitual fatigue of the gross body is dangerous since it conditions the subtle body to drowsiness. This in turn conditions the gross body to the dulling forces which snuff out spiritual life and higher perception. Fatigue must be endured periodically but it should not become a habit. I noticed that when we are thoroughly fatigued we sleep like logs, just like dense matter. We sleep in such a way that we do not remember anything but our lack of memory does not protect us from having spiritually-destructive relations or intoxicating experiences. It simply means that it deactivated memory, dulled memory, disengaged discrimination and turned us into unconscious beings on the subtle plane. This is not to our benefit nor is it our aim.

Since we are so heavily conditioned in material existence and since in the general sense, our conditioning continues full force with flashes of enlightenment here and there, our liberation is uncertain. The question is: When will any of us be completely liberated? We have tried life after life, only to find ourselves in another material body in another time phase, again endeavoring endlessly. When will we break the cycle of haphazard, uncontrollable birth and death? It is obvious that liberation must be awarded for we simply cannot achieve it by our own effort.

The subtle body needs to be curbed because it is impulsively inclined. Just as we find ourselves in this gross body now, at the time of death we will find ourselves in the subtle dream form. As we now deal with the habits of this gross body such as urination, sexual expression and evacuation, we will have to deal with the habits of the subtle body at the time of death. Thus one should try by all means to realize that body and curb it.

The subtle body is under the influence of previous activities, and it is easily swayed by emotional pulls. Let us consider the case of a married man. He is married and due to religious principles he does not take another wife. He is tempted when he meets desirable women but he resists. However in dreams, his subtle body may not follow the moral aims. It may sexually engage with other women since it is easier to follow moral principles on the physical level than on the subtle one.

The subtle body is uninhibited or unrestrained and unless we make a deliberate effort to curb it, it is hardly likely that we would act with a strong sense of discrimination in the subtle world. Due to its sensuous nature, the subtle body is emotionally inclined and resistant to sense control.

Habituation to rebirth is a tendency of the subtle body. It is a very strong habit that is extremely difficult to overcome. It is so difficult that many who desire transit to higher worlds or who plan to do so on the basis of religious faith, also deeply rely on the rebirth tendency of the subtle body. If given the opportunity to actually go higher, they could not take it, because the rebirth tendency of the subtle body will pull them back to this world.

Salvation really means that God frees us and we free ourselves simultaneously. It never means that God frees us as we remain stagnant. That is not possible. God, for all He is, cannot free us if we do not try to free ourselves in the process. Our participation is required because we are individual entities with individual resolution and initiative.

Krishna established that existentially, once a person comes into being as an individual entity, there is no question of his individuality being lost at any time. It is a permanent feature for eternity. In addition, Krishna said that our position in the hereafter is mainly determined by the concepts of life we maintained habitually.

The rebirth tendency of the subtle body deals with rejuvenation of the life force in the body. The life force is usually stationed at the base of the spinal column in the body, near the sexual and excretory areas. After staying in a body until it ages and becomes diseased, the life force is fatigued considerably.

Since the life force engages the limbs, senses and organs in involuntary actions, and since it controls the breathing system as well, it eventually gets fatigued, especially when the body becomes diseased and worn out. Thus the life force, which becomes attached to the body and wants to protect it even if the body is fatally wounded or terminally ill, desires to get a new gross body. This tendency for getting infant forms is strongly rooted in the subtle form of which the life force is a part. It is very difficult to get rid of this tendency.

When the body gets old and worn out it requires care from nurses, relatives, doctors and friends. Therefore it develops an attitude of dependence on others. At the time, we assess our lives, raking and scraping through the stockpile of memories to see which persons are obligated. Children and grandchildren are obligated; non-related dependents are obligated and friends as well. If we have money, we pay a doctor and he becomes obligated. Thus we develop a very unhealthy and materialistic attitude toward life, and out of desperation, we demand services from others. These tendencies are all part of the transmigration habit. If we do not take practical steps to remove ourselves from this habit, we will definitely take another body.

If one passes from this world, looking to the people here to assist one with an old worn-out body, one will more than likely return to this world to be someone's child. As an infant, one will continue getting the services one received prior to passing from the last body. What are these services? Let us consider.

If we visit any hospital or home for the aged or encounter a person with an elderly body who lives at home, we see the general need for help to clean the elderly body, to eat, go to bed, wake up and so on. Just as a baby body requires help to clean waste matter that is expelled, an elderly body often requires assistance with bed pans and urine receptacles. As a baby is checked by a doctor, so a person with an aged body must be checked frequently. As a baby is fed milk or mashed foods by the mother, so the elderly are fed special diets due to their poor digestive ability. As a baby is preoccupied with soft stools, so the elderly are plagued with constipation and hard stools. Therefore we find a connection between the elderly condition and the infantile one which follows immediately after the transition to the next body.

The subtle body is attached to rebirth and the gross one is attached to survival. Since survival is limited and one's body can only survive for a limited number of years, the subtle body is naturally adaptive to moving on to other bodies. It is so rooted that we become resistant to the idea of having a permanent spiritual form. As animals like to roam from place to place, so the subtle body likes to move from body to body. We are conditioned by long association with that subtle form.

Once it is kicked out of a body, the main concern of the life force is to find another body by getting into the genitals of a man for implantation into a woman's body and that is the sum and substance of the transmigration process. As simple as it sounds, it is one of the most difficult tendencies to overcome.

The life force is so attached to returning to this world in a baby form that it supports social situations in the hope that in the next body it will take advantage of the society it helped to establish. Let us take the example of a doctor. He establishes a medical practice. Then his body dies. But the story does not end there because the life force directs him to enter the genitals of his son or grandson, so that he again returns to become a doctor, to enjoy the prestige he established in the previous life.

A rich merchant who passes away, tries his best to return as a son or grandson in the same family, so that as a child he can enjoy growing up in a wealthy family. He feels very comfortable in such a setting because he endeavored for it in the former life.

These tendencies of ours cannot be eliminated merely by having faith in God. We must also endeavor to rid ourselves of these deep-seated urges. The faith is necessary and it should be there but it must be activated by a cleansing process now, before the time of death; otherwise the faith alone will be insufficient to free us.

Our reluctance to take up cleansing actions is linked with confidence in the process of birth and death. This confidence is based on the subtle body which is the foundation or basis of the soul's journey from one body to another in total psychic blindness. Though we forget the process, our confidence in it remains. When one enters an aircraft to go to a distant city, he may be seated in such a way that he cannot see where the aircraft travels. Still he is confident that the machine will arrive at the destination safely. For all practical purposes, he is blind during the flight. He only sees if he survives and leaves the craft to disembark. Similarly, after death and while in a mother's womb, one becomes blind, but he gets vision again when he is delivered from the mother's belly. Still, his lack of vision or understanding of the hereafter does not in any way damage his sense of confidence in the transmigration process. His lack of memory of former births does not deprive him of the urge to stay close to relatives after death, so that he can again enter a would-be father's body for another chance at earthly life.

One may follow whatever religion and whatever spiritual master suits one's fancy, but if the authority is unable to convince one to become purified, one will again return to another material body in the same transmigratory way. This is the process of psychic nature and merely following a religion or an established spiritual master does not guarantee change.

Since we know deep inside, even deeper than our conscious memory, that we will get another earthly body, sooner or later after death, why should we try for complete purification? What is the hurry? Why not continue in the usual way of professing a certain faith, dying to another body, getting a new body thereafter, taking to religion or being atheistic again and repeating a familiar history life after life?

Generally we forget the past life and we become aware of past memories as predispositions and instincts. An example can be given. A certain boy wanted to play music. His parents sent him to a music teacher. No other boy in that village of thirty boys wanted to learn music. Some wanted to learn carpentry. However, the boy with the music inclination went to the teacher and he quickly learnt music. This is a form of memory, where he subconsciously remembered that he cultivated the music art in the past life. The other boys who wanted to be carpenters were also subconsciously remembering their cultivation of building skills from the past. This is how we usually remember past lives.

A few rare souls do remember the past life objectively but generally that is not possible. Memory of past lives is greatly dependent on how we passed from the last body. If we were careless, we will not remember.

Chapter 9

The Time of Death

Rejection of material bodies or the desire not to have any, is for the most part a desire only and not an actual possibility, for in fact we do not have the power to stop ourselves from transmigrating. It is a natural process for conditioned entities. Until we are completely purified and freed from the rebirth tendency, the process continues uninterruptedly, no matter what we hope or think.

In the northern countries, the frost comes and the leaves fall to the ground. It does not matter if the trees like the idea or if observers like the animals and humans, like it either. It is the process of nature which must undoubtedly be tolerated by the trees and inhabitants. In the same way the transmigration process is in vogue as the unalterable way of this world.

At the time of death the brain goes dead. In medical terminology this is called cerebral or brain death. In this event the brain is no longer effective and does not respond to willpower. If the soul, the thinker, enters such a state, even if he tries to wake up the body, it will not become conscious because the brain cannot transmit his desire. While the body is alive in good health and even during times of disease, the brain acts as an agent to transmit desire through a series of nerves but once the brain dies, that transmission stops. Sometimes only a part of the brain dies and this is called a stroke. If the whole brain stops transmitting, it is understood to be a complete stroke or coma, and if the remaining bodily organs also stop or lose all health, it is called death. At that point one can no longer communicate through the body. The thinker or soul who inhabited the body does not stop communicating but at that point the body no longer functions as medium for communication. Subtle communication continues but the gross communication that was relayed through the body stops.

The problem with brain death is that it signifies cessation of an entire cluster of memories. This is because we habitually rely on the brain to store recorded information. This is illustrated by our tendency as human beings to keep records of all sorts. In any government office there are records of information. There are paper and electronic means of information. This media storage indicates that we rely on help from material nature to retain memory of events. If we rely on a mere piece of paper, we can just imagine how much we rely on the brain. If we lose a piece of paper that carries an important fact, we may lose the information entirely and in the same way when the brain is dead, we lose a whole set of memories which we are unable to carry to the next life.

However not all events are stored in the brain in memory form. Some are stored in the subtle body in the form of tendencies, likes and dislikes, attractions and aversions. Some are stored in the form of tiny pictures and sounds, like the sound waves that are projected through space and are converted by a radio receiver or television. However these memories of the subtle body are also imperiled if we pass away in anxiety or without mystic perception and psychic purification.

At the time of death, one must, all of a sudden, change priorities. One may not want to but one must. All ideas which are based on having a gross body are drastically reduced at the time of death. Let us take the instance of the traveler who boards an aircraft. Once he enters the craft, the door is locked. After the engines are fired by the pilot and the airplane taxies down the runway, the traveler cannot change his mind. Suppose he wants to go back and get his *Bible* or *Bhagavad Gītā*. He cannot. He will not be allowed. The aircraft steward will simply say, "Sir, I am sorry. The aircraft is closed and the interior spaces are pressurized. It cannot be opened until we land safely."

At the time of death, if we forget spiritual knowledge or if we did not pay sufficient attention during life to retain the essentials, we will not be able to increase spiritual adeptness or knowledge one fraction.

Now let us assume that the aircraft leaves the runway and rises thousands of feet in the air. This is like going to heaven or like having a nice experience of going in the preferred direction for a better body in the next life. But suppose all of a sudden there is an explosion. The pilot loses control of the aircraft. What next? What should the passenger do? What can he do?

At that moment of the explosion, all passengers are vulnerable. They must all forget current affairs and think seriously of their risky condition. So at the time of death, one must leave everything and think seriously. One may not listen to a mystic while alive and a passenger may not listen to an official who explains the procedure to use a parachute or escape chute in case of danger. Nevertheless, in a crisis, one is forced to consider.

While we have a healthy body we may not care. We are confident. Things go smoothly. The family progresses. The circle of friends increases. The business prospers. The wallet is full. In such a circumstance, who cares? Death? What is that? Only those who are terminally-ill need consider imminent death. But when death approaches, even in youth, one has no alternative but to face the task.

One passenger on the aircraft took the precaution of securing life insurance before traveling but even in his case, what was the outcome? A person with life insurance is like a religious man who professes faith but who is not purified enough to cash in on the assured policies of his religion. Actually, each of us is like that passenger. Each of us failed in the past life and now we are back with our adolescent attitude towards religion, feeling that a higher destination in the hereafter awaits us. We are the same people with the same sense of imaginary confidence. We are again being lazy in the task of spiritual advancement.

Then there is another passenger, who thought of his girlfriend and looked at her picture when the explosion occurred. The picture was sucked out of his hand by the release of cabin pressure. Besides that, he no longer thinks of her. He was forced to change priorities. It was a matter of his life or death. Similarly, after death, one changes priorities. One no longer gives a hoot about the so-called loved ones. At that time one simply worries about one's lost life and one's longing to be part of this social scene.

And the loneliness, to know that the explosion might mean death, severe injury or suffering which I, the passenger, may face. What to do? Where is the assistance of friends and relatives? Where is the insurance representative?

After death, one must view life from a new perspective, in an entirely different way. One must make association with the authorities and inhabitants of the hereafter. One must also know how to get into a father's body or must at least have the natural skill to do so. Otherwise one enters into a state of uncertainty, anxiety and panic.

As the man must forget his girlfriend and establish relationships with fellow passengers and the flight attendants, as he must forget his boss and take orders from the pilot, so at the time of death we lose sight and memory of acquaintances.

A priest, spiritual master, pastor or counselor may say what he likes while in a healthy body but after death deprives him of the form, such a person may be unable to assist himself or his followers. These very leaders might have to rely on others. For instance, a Christian pastor might be restricted to taking rebirth in a Hindu family. As a child in a Hindu home, he would be indoctrinated into a totally different concept of religion, worshiping idols that he rejected in the past life. A man in a white body might find that he must take shelter in the semen of a black man, to come out in the next life in a black colored body and thus be subjected to insults and intimidations that are given to such a body in a white-oriented society. Such are the contrary circumstances which might possibly confront one after death of the current body.

After death, who will help the person who fails in the bid for salvation and must again take another earthly form? Will my spiritual master or my priest get me a body in a family whose faith is compatible with my past life, or will I have to take an undesirable body?

One's sense of language, culture and national orientation may be totally shattered after death, as one may have to take birth in a foreign country and thereby be forced to assume different habits. Most of all one may have to change the entire way of relating in order to be adopted by the new set of parents. One typically has to change character, methods and behavior to get the affection of a particular family to be their child.

For an advanced entity, rebirth may be a lowering experience whereby one takes birth in a family that has little or no spiritual practices. Such a birth is preferable to birth in the animal world or to a prolonged stay in a confused state on the astral levels, but it implies that one must strive for elevation and regain spiritual order after one gets the body. In such a situation, one must first serve time as a child before continuing spiritual discipline from the previous life.

Further, if one takes such a birth and does not understand that he was lowered, there is every chance that one will not get back on course, but will cling to childhood traditions and thus stagnate and become lost to spiritual glory from previous lives.

At the time of death one's education becomes imperiled. When the soul is displaced from the body, it no longer cares for education and influence. It no longer cares about status of a doctor, lawyer, laborer, president or clerk. At that time the priority is to get another earthly form. Usually religious people feel that they are better situated than those who attend no church, mosque or temple but at the time of death every human being, religious or nonreligious, becomes very much concerned about getting another earthly body. It is only the very rare liberated souls who are not in anxiety regarding the loss of an earthly form.

Religious folk feel that they are going to heaven or to the kingdom of God or that they will merge into a superb type of happiness after death. Instead of looking for heaven or trying to reach that vague and unknown place, they usually make effort to reawaken in this earthly place just as before in the early morning hours of every day. When they find that they are unable, they try to contact relatives and friends to express helplessness. This earthly world is their heaven.

On the other hand the nonreligious people, those who are careless and superstitious or those who feel that there is no God and no soul, realize that they continue to exist anyway, except that their most important tool of communication, the human body, is missing. They also attempt to return to the physical plane. The fact remains that regardless of religious affiliation, if one does not cultivate the self spiritually, it is hardly likely that one will go to a heaven hereafter. One will experience the hereafter as no more than shifting subtle scenes just as one experiences it consciously or unconsciously every night in dreams.

Some religious faiths say that the ungodly will see hell and the ungodly scoff at the idea but it is a fact that we feel and see hell in this earthly life as well as in dreams and in the hereafter. Hells like those described in religious scriptures do exist. It is proven every day in this troublesome earthly life and every night in the shifty, ghostly, nightmarish dream life. Just as we are inconvenienced impersonally in this life, so we might suffer impersonally in the hereafter, without understanding who is punishing us or why. When there is an earthquake or a terrible storm, we see no one but nature as the cause, even though supernatural entities might be adjusting nature to inconvenience us. In the same way we may be punished in the hereafter in hellish conditions without understanding who wields the discipline.

Once the departed soul gets a new body, its instinct is to regain the money, property, education and power it possessed in the former life. One may get some money but one finds that one cannot repossess sufficient wealth. As for education, one finds that one has to learn almost everything all over again by going to school for years in childhood and adolescence. If one does not learn or if one subconsciously resents being schooled, one becomes a disgruntled dunce, a rejected member of society. One fails to re-possess the former status as a doctor, lawyer or industrialist. One then takes to bad company and takes up vices like liquor drinking, cigarette smoking, narcotics consumption, and irresponsible sexual acts. Thus one degrades the self.

Once the soul gets a new body, he or she meets former acquaintances and dependents from past lives. Even though one does not consciously remember, one's subconscious memory functions as a liking and disliking instinct.

In the next life, when experiencing rejection of one's ideas and frustration of one's objectives, one rethinks the situation. One concludes that either God is crazy or nature is totally disorganized but the truth is that one is unrealistic and lacks insight. One may strive to adjust destiny but one finds frustration, except in those areas facilitated by providence.

If one wants to improve when one gets an infant form, one has to prepare in the present life by adjusting the haughty, presumptuous mentality towards destiny. One should begin thinking of the next life and seriously, in a cool-headed mood, one must analyze honestly if one actually wants to go to heaven or to a higher world of one's choice. One should assess one's actual qualifications by checking daily activities. Qualifications of religious faith are insufficient for we are promoted to higher worlds on the basis of behavior, elevated tendencies and ability to resist vices on all levels.

One may be rich in this life and take birth in poverty in the next. In that case if one desires a reputation for wealth, one would have to give up resentment and work in an enterprising way to acquire fortune. One may be rich in this life on the basis of having received an education in childhood, but in the next life even if one takes birth in a wealthy family, one still has to get an education all over again. Therefore, one could prepare the self for this by maintaining a study attitude throughout life and thereby keep the subtle body interested in learning. Then in the next life as an infant, one would have an easy time progressing through schools. It requires a little thinking but we can prepare ourselves for the next life.

As far as seeing hell in the hereafter, that is quite likely and possible but as I stated, we may not see the controller of the hellish sufferings. In other words, even in this world a criminal may never see a high court judge who passes down the sentence. He may never see the warden-in-chief of the prison compound during the jail term. Some dangerous prisoners are taken blindfolded, handcuffed and strapped before a judge. They are escorted while blindfolded, into the prison compound. Likewise, one does not always see hell objectively or see the judge in the subtle world of the departed. That authority is as real as any police or judicial authority in this world, but we may not see it. Thus in the next life we may not believe those who tell us that we will be judged immediately after death.

The supernatural people who inflict punishments in the form of unexplained accidents, natural disasters and widespread diseases are not seen with our common eyes but one who has mystic vision may perceive them.

I assure readers that there is hell in the hereafter but it is not like the Christian idea of a perpetual or eternal hell. It is hell for a limited time period. One is released from it to continue existence in the normal way. Hell is certain if we commit criminal acts but it will not last forever.

Once I was taken in my subtle body to the hell for butchers. I was taken there just to give testimony for the publication of this book, just as a modern news reporter might be given a tour of a prison block, so that he can write an eyewitness report. When one gets to that hellish place, he gets there in his dream body but he feels as if he is in the physical form. Since the dream form looks and feels like the earthly body, one thinks that he is in a physical world. Therefore the hereafter experience is felt to be as real as earthly existence.

According to the Vedic literatures, the controller of the hell is *Yamarāja* and he is described in the Vedic text as having a red-eyed, resplendent blackish body which is adorned with a turban and yellow robe. However the superintendent of the place I visited was in a whitish body which had a yellowish hue. The particular section of hell that I was shown was a death camp, a very dismal place. The superintendent had helpers who were mean-looking, human-like beings. They were expert in hurting the subtle bodies of the prisoners. A particular man who recently departed his earthly form and who as a criminal in his earthly life had stabbed victims while taking their money, was held by guards while the superintendent took a sharp knife and ran it through his chest. The man felt great pain and then his subtle body fainted. After this he was revived and the wound and pain were gone but all the while the departed criminal remembered the events of his former vicious lifestyle.

I then asked the superintendent how he enlisted the helpers who serve as ghost police. He replied, "These assistants were criminals in former lives. They used to kill people dispassionately. Now they are trained in how to use violence judicially. This orients them to assume positions as policemen or soldiers in the next life. They have the killing tendency. It cannot be rooted out easily. Through this association, they learn how to apply themselves constructively. When they return to the earthly society, they will desire to use violence for the welfare of society."

After this I wanted to ask other questions and be allowed to see other parts of that hellish territory. The place appeared to be extensive and divided into various sections like an entire planet of hellish regions. However, I was not allowed. My subtle body returned to the gross one which was sleeping in Mississippi on this earthly place.

Materialistic people usually hesitate to accept reincarnation of the soul into earthly bodies but it is reality. We can see clearly the habit of reincarnation even in those who do not believe in the rebirth process. Their attachment to children and grandchildren is evidence that they want to return into the family line through the body of a descendant. Invariably we see that most people remain attached even to naughty, disagreeable and dishonorable children and grandchildren. This tendency is strong evidence of reincarnation whereby the impulsive tendency of the subtle body forms relationships with an underlying motive to secure future parents. In fact, the sure way for any of these people to avoid hell is to remain attached to a family member who might beget a body quickly, as soon as one leaves the old worn-out earthly form. One way to avoid the ghost police is by taking shelter in the body of a relative immediately after death. If one becomes lodged in a would-be parent body immediately after death, the ghost police are unable to arrest one, as one would fuse in the bloodstream and feelings of that relative.

In the Indian legend of Satyavan and Savitri, it is related that Satyavan's body was destined to die at a young age. This meant that his subtle body was to permanently separate from the gross one in youth. However Satyavan married and became attached to his wife. When his gross body died, his wife petitioned the death controller to release his subtle form. Her wish was granted. In other words, after the body dies, one may avoid the death controller if one can somehow or other take shelter with a relative.

In the legend of Ajamil, he passed from an old worn-out and diseased material body but since he had a criminal record and was vice-ridden, he was wanted by ghost police. However at the time of death, Ajamila instinctively called his son. He tried to reach his son in order to take shelter with the living. By taking shelter in a living relative, one may avoid the ghost police. This does not mean that one can do this life after life indefinitely. One may do this in one or two lives but then one may be arrested and punished for cumulative crimes against mankind, nature and God Almighty.

Attachment of elderly people to youngsters signified a sense of needing new bodies. It is an instinctive urge to prepare us to accept one of our descendants as the next parent. This is the evidence of our subtle body's strong tendency for reincarnation. Unless this tendency is rooted out and we become detached, there is no question of going to any higher world, because at the time of death, our tendency of attachment will pull us back to this world. Thus religious faith is nullified if we remain attached socially.

Reincarnation is mostly a problem for those whose gross bodies died and who require new earthly forms, but who are unable to become settled in the bloodstream of a human being. However rebirth is also a problem for those who are alive. Those who are living will, in the future, be required to permanently leave the present gross forms. Besides this, they are mentally and emotionally harassed by the souls who hover in the astral world or who entered their bloodstream or subtle body for rebirth as children.

The influence of children in one's life is not always positive. It is rarely conducive to spiritual advancement. Those who want bodies are for the most part materialistic, at least those in the lower astral atmosphere. Their influence makes one more and more insensitive to spiritual views. Thus if one has an obligation to any of them, one should fulfill the obligation without jeopardizing spiritual advancement. It is for this reason that many ascetics avoid begetting and focus on celibacy.

After trying life after life to be responsible parents and finding that the responsibility of householder life usually concludes in spiritual digression, they run or shy away from such a life. One has to be very perceptive, and very powerful to be a householder and simultaneously make noteworthy spiritual advancement. Most of the souls to whom one may be obligated in the begetting process are materialistic. They influence one's mind, emotions and body in a non-spiritual direction. They use one's energy to reinforce materialistic and sensual desires which are counterproductive in the spiritual sense.

One should prepare for the death of the body. That is important. If one keeps in mind that he must by all means leave the body sooner or later, it will be easy to prepare and be mindful. If not, one will forget that destiny will kill the body and one will be caught off guard when the time comes.

Householders should prepare for death by becoming detached from loved ones without being irresponsible towards them. One should maintain family responsibilities as far as possible but should be detached all the same. When separated from a loved one in the routine course of life on a daily, weekly, monthly or yearly basis, one should be responsible towards that person but should not overindulge in longing to be with the said relative. One should maintain the responsibilities in a pleasant but detached attitude. A responsible householder should have two concerns:

- *responsibilities to a household*
- *personal spiritual advancement*

These two aspects should develop side by side without the spiritual life being imperiled or neglected altogether.

For advanced meditation one should gain control over the life force in the body and curtail its impulsive activity. One can realize the life force by studying the way the body defends itself. For instance, there are involuntary movements and actions which are performed without our expressed will. These actions are executed by the life force, thus establishing the life force as a distinct indispensible function.

In the *Bhagavad Gītā* Śrī Krishna gave us some idea of how we can realize this life force even without taking up the *prāṇāyāma* yoga practice which gives yogis the ability to recognize this distinct and separate power in the body.

Describing the psychology of an advanced mystic, He said:

- *"I do not initiate anything." Being proficient in yoga, this is what the knower of reality thinks. While seeing, hearing, touching, smelling, eating, walking, sleeping and breathing,*

- *...while talking, evacuating, holding, opening and closing the eyelids, he considers, "The senses are interlocked with the attractive objects." (Bhagavad Gītā 5.8-9)*

One who knows reality and understands the different situations and energies of the body, realizes everything through his sense of detachment from it. By deep consideration he understands that visual perception, hearing tendency, touching ability, smelling power, eating ability, mobility, sleeping tendency and breathing function go on automatically to a greater degree. That person realizes that the core-self does not control these functions absolutely. In speaking, evacuating, grasping and operating the eyelids, that person knows that the material senses are being motivated to interact with material objects and the soul is aloof from this process.

The body is driven by the life force and not by the mind which resides in the head of the body. The life force resides in the spinal column of the average man, at the base of it, near the genital and anal area. With a little detachment one can begin to perceive this driving force. It motivates or goads the mind. The mind in turn drives the senses to act for procurement of sense gratification and for defense of the body. It is said that the mind is engaged essentially in two activities, namely, accepting and rejecting or grasping and pushing away. It grasps whatever it senses would satisfy the body and it pushes away whatever appears to be detrimental. Actually the decisions are not made by the mind. They are executed by the life force which is underneath the mind. This force makes costly mistakes in its impulsive activities.

Since a particular soul is tagged for all the mistakes of its life force, it is in the person's interest to get that force under control and to censure its activities so that it operates sensibly. In the beginning of the meditation practice, one tries to get the mind under control and one succeeds to a degree but one realizes sooner or later that there is another energy that pushes the mind impulsively even against one's wishes. This energy is the life force. Persons who study the *rāja* yoga process eventually realize that they must find a way to control the life force. In ancient times, the *prāṇāyāma* method was used because if the breath is controlled the life force is disempowered, since it draws energy from the air we breathe. It is just like lion-taming. To tame a lion, one must capture the animal and keep it confined in a cave, pit or cage. Then one must control-feed the animal and gradually the creature is subdued.

However the life force can also be controlled by the method of observing its impulsive activities. If we study carefully we will see that a simple matter like digestion of foodstuffs is beyond our control. It goes on automatically. This automation is being conducted by the life force. All physiological aspects and functions are conducted by the life force, either in our interest or against it. If for instance the body is addicted to sweets, I may not be able to reduce the body's sugar intake if the life force is strongly addicted. Therefore the life force must be curbed at all costs. The mind is merely a stooge of the life force and even if one gets the mind focused, as soon as there is an impulse from the sneaky life force, the mind will deviate.

In spiritual life, one makes a bid to control the gross body but then one finds that the mind and emotions are unruly. Therefore one tries to control the mind and its contents by forcibly engaging it in services which it dislikes but which are in one's interest. As soon as one begins to force the mind one feels that progress is made but then one becomes intensely aware of feelings and emotions that resist rigid control. At this point one must stop and reconsider.

Consider sexual indulgence for example. A householder may make a mental decision with all due reason and concern for his spiritual life to stop all whimsical sexual indulgence. Similarly a monk may decide that he does not want to masturbate to expel semen. Still, these mental decisions are not sufficient because the mind is not an absolute authority in the body. Behind the mind is the life force which conducts feelings, emotions and impulsive actions.

Ordinarily, the life force is completely independent and commands the gross and subtle body to its preference. Let us continue here with our example of sexual control. The householder made a decision to stop whimsical sex life but when he next encounters his wife and finds her to be in a romantic mood, his heart melts, his mind catches the mood and he is escorted through a range of pleasurable feelings until driven to expel semen in her body. On the other hand, the monk discovers that he cannot stop himself from masturbating as if masturbation was like evacuation, which is a mandatory activity of the body.

These impulsive acts are directed by the life force. They are not haphazard. They are controlled by a particular force in the body, namely the life force.

Of course, the life force must cooperate with the mind and the soul in the body. It cannot work alone. Still, the life force steals energy from the soul and drives the mind in a hidden way that is hardly realized by the average human being. Let us take the example of evacuation. That is, of course, a mandatory function. Even though we may decide not to emit semen from the body, we cannot make the decision not to pass waste from it. Therefore our decision-making is limited. We cannot decide not to breathe. Again, in so many respects, the life force has the advantage. If perchance one feels the call of nature to evacuate, he can stall for a time.

He does not have to evacuate immediately unless his body is sick and has diarrhea. If the body is well he can stall the call of nature, or in other words, he can resist the instruction of the life force which is being realized by the impulse to pass stools. However, as soon as he makes the decision to delay the passage of stools, the life force stops pressuring him to evacuate and begins to maintain the stools in the body. Therefore, the person's decision to ignore nature's call to evacuate was made at the expense of his body's health.

In such aspects as evacuation, it is definitely beneficial to cooperate with the life force but in other aspects it is foolish and harmful to go along with the impulses. To make the proper decisions one has to study how the life force operates and then learn how to regulate it.

Mind and sense control are the beginnings of yoga practice. Those who fail to realize the life force cannot possibly reach the advanced stages because the life force will continue pilfering energy to engage in costly impulsive acts.

We may inquire as to why the mind is easily located in the brain area and the emotions are easily recognized in the brain, chest and pubic regions but the life force in the base of the spinal column is so difficult to perceive. The answer is that the brain has the most sensitive nerves. Due to that sensitivity, we can perceive the mind easily. Similarly, strong feelings of love and emotion which arise from the chest region are triggered easily and so they are located by feelings. The life force, on the other hand, is in an area with less nerve sensitivity, making it extremely difficult to discern.

For the average human, the life force is realized in sex expression only. This force does many things to maintain the body while the soul lives in the body and enjoys faculties. Usually a spirit uses a body for many years and only perceives the life force at the beginning of the body and at the end when the body dies. Otherwise the self expresses no interest in the life force. The self is careless in that way. Its sole concern is to use the body for sensual enjoyment and exploitation. Its interest is reduced to political supremacy and sexual indulgence.

In sexual indulgence, the enlivening power which one experiences as pleasure is the super-charged life force. A few of its less obvious and less intensive expressions are when the body belches through the mouth or expels gas through the anus. It is also felt when one is thirsty and then becomes satisfied by the ingestion of water, or when the body is fatigued and drifts effortlessly into a state of restful sleep. Nevertheless, the most intense and forceful expression takes place through sexual gratification. This is how the average man can undoubtedly recognize and realize the life force.

A tiger cannot be tamed so long as it remains in its jungle area, where it is quite familiar with the territory and where it is the chief predator. The hunter has to flush the animal out, trap it, starve it, feed it by regulation and then tame it. Like this, the life force must be flushed out of the lower portion of the body and its activities must be closely watched and censored in the interest of the soul; otherwise liberation will be forestalled.

Any process that does not penetrate deeply into our nature cannot at any stage set us free from the modes of material nature. It is simply not possible because material nature will keep hiding and influencing us from the subconscious level. The process must be powerful enough to penetrate the subconscious.

Chapter 10

Control of the Life Force through Mystic Technique

The life force can be controlled through mystic techniques as well as through certain breathing exercises and muscular locks used in yoga. Actually the yogis who are expert, utilize all three methods simultaneously. These are not very difficult techniques but they appear to be so because we are unfamiliar with them.

Until we reach the stage of realizing that materialistic living is against our spiritual constitution, we cannot effectively corner the life force. It is the force that sponsors materialistic desires. If we cling to mundane desires, we cannot tame that energy but will remain in a situation of being impulsively driven and blackmailed by pleasure and vices. So long as we are looking for any pleasure in some corner of the material creation, we will remain in bondage.

Yogis and other seekers speak of mind control as being essential but only the yogis speak of life force control. This is because life force control cannot be attained by neophytes. It is too subtle of an accomplishment. It is not difficult but it is very subtle. It is discussed when one reaches an advanced stage.

Mind control usually begins with control of the external activities of the senses but this is only the beginning. Nevertheless some spiritual societies advocate this as the complete process. In the beginning one is asked to take vows or to make promises to follow certain rules and regulations such as no flesh eating, no liquor drinking or taking of intoxicants, no sexual indulgence except with a spouse, and no gambling. There are other rules but these are the essential ones. A single man or woman who lives at a spiritual center is asked not to speak with sexual overtones. These rules are mostly external guidelines which introduce one to mind control by means of restraining the senses and limbs of the gross body.

The yogi who begins like this, quickly finds out that even though he is encouraged on the external level, his inner mind and feelings violate the rules. He feels the need for a better, more complete system of control which keeps the inner nature within the regulations.

The gross and subtle bodies are different and the various parts of each of these bodies are also different. Thus the control of these bodies requires special attention. If the engine of a car is faulty, one cannot fix it by fixing the tires. And if the mind is faulty, the mind has to be fixed directly. In a general way, one can fix the mind by a bodily treatment but when there is an acute problem, the mind itself must be tended.

To control the mind, one should learn how to rest and shut down the mind. To shut off the mind one should learn how to withdraw one's spiritual power or attention from the mind and this has little to do with the physical body. This is purely a concern of the subtle body since the mind is the brain of that body. If one has a headache, he should treat the head not the toe.

At first one must feel within and sense how psychological power surges through the mind from the core-self.

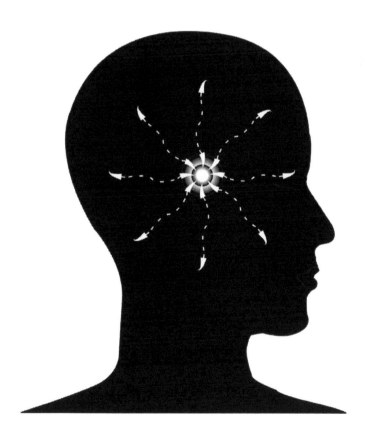

Next, one must try to pull back the outward-directed power into the core-self.

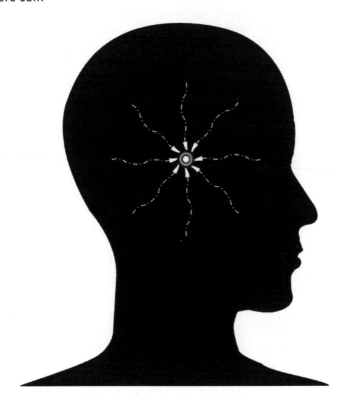

When one learns to do this, one should do it with closed eyes in a reclined position or in any comfortable position without noise in the environment.

One will feel as if the power that surges out of the core-self is drawn back into it, just as streams which flow from a lake may begin flowing back into the lake, if there is an earthquake and the land rises.

This is the process of de-energizing the mind. Until one has mastered this, one cannot make substantial progress in controlling and restricting the mind. One should directly sever the mind's power and bring it under control. In the Bhagavad Gītā, there is a verse that describes this withdrawn condition more accurately.

- *When such a person pulls fully out of moods, he or she may be compared to the tortoise with its limbs retracted. The senses are withdrawn from the attractive things in the case of a person whose reality-piercing vision is established. (Bhagavad Gītā 2.58)*

Once the mind is de-energized and one practices this for sometime, one begins to realize that the mind is only partially at fault in the sense that it expands or amplifies one's desires. One begins to see that the fault is not really in the mind but in the core-self. At this point one should introspect and get help from a more advanced meditator. By the process of pulling back the expressive powers of the core-self, one increases spiritual perception.

Once the mind and core-self are treated in this manner, one can tackle the life force. One cannot tackle it in the beginning because it is hidden too deeply at the base of the spinal column, but as soon as one sharpens mystic perception, one can tackle that great power which commands the psyche with such authority.

Regardless of whether one is a yogi, or a person lacking interest in spiritual life, the life force will have a feeble glow if the lower body is contaminated. This occurs in the subtle and gross bodies as well. The general condition of the gross body tells us much about the situation of the subtle form.

Feeble Glow of Life Force

As one advances and as that portion of the body is charged with fresh energy, the blood circulation improves and the liquid solar energy circulation improves in the subtle form. The life force becomes brilliant and it rises up the spine, clearing away the usual darkness that surrounds it on all sides.

Life Force Penetrates Spinal Column

When this occurs the attitude of the life force changes. Its lower tendencies go away permanently to such an extent that the person concerned is rarely bothered by lower impulses. He or she no longer has to make an effort for restraint from spiritually-destructive sensual acts. As for sexual involvement, that tendency is erased from the mind and body; the person no longer has to make an effort to be celibate. As for diet, the person eats less and gets just as much energy out of less food and out of lighter foods that are acquired without violence.

To others the person appears to be austere but within the self he or she feels that the new lifestyle is natural. In Sanskrit it is said that a transcendentalist in this condition is being influenced by pranotthana or the release of pranic solarized energy which activates the brow chakra (third eye) and opens the crown chakra (mystic hole at top of head).

When the brow chakra is opened one begins to see mystically, is more aware of foreign thoughts, and becomes increasingly conscious of dream contacts. When the crown chakra is fully open, one perceives and communicates with the celestial people who must ultimately assist one in the bid for liberation. This state of purification cannot be bypassed. It is mandatory preparation for a higher life in the hereafter upon the death of one's body.

Release of Pranotthana (Solarized Energy)

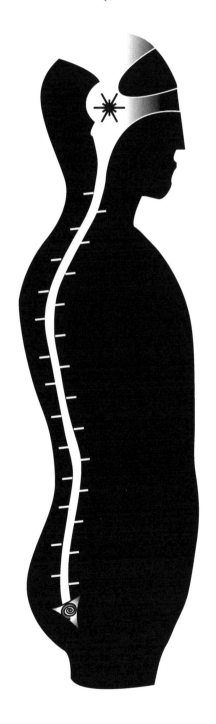

It is important to understand that regardless of a man's position in society, he will not be able to brighten his life force if he is habituated to constipation, or delayed evacuation of stools, or if his body stores much semen in the groin area rather than releasing it into the bloodstream continually, or if the blood circulation in the buttocks, thighs, groin and feet is poor. His life force will be dull because it will be used up mostly in the lower part of the body. This does not mean that he will not aspire. If he is a transcendentalist he certainly will but his life force will not cooperate fully with higher ideals because it is dutifully preoccupied in the lower trunk and thighs of the body.

Since every entity is individual and since every one of us has initiative, we must invest our determination in spiritual elevation. Otherwise we will remain in the material situation with animal consciousness, life after life.

No one attains salvation by the lazy method of avoiding purification and spiritual advancement. It is not possible. Some individual effort is required for salvation. Of course, if one has no transcendental impetus, it is better to keep faith in God and to affiliate oneself with a spiritual society but that does not mean that one will gain release from material existence.

Even though you have faith in God, where is your determination going? Where is your initiative being placed? Where do you endeavor the most? The answer is that the area one endeavors in the most, develops the most. The direction of the endeavoring ability elevates or degrades us and thereby creates our direction in the next life.

The living being has energy but he is limited at best. If he uses the energy efficiently, the spiritual faculties may increase.

If the energy is dissipated in social and subtle vices, one cannot experience anything but mental darkness. Even in the most ignorant condition one can have faith in God but the determination to relate to divine beings in an elevated way will not manifest if one has little energy to invest in religion and devotion.

The psychic and mystic faculties are natural properties of the spiritual soul, just as walking, talking, seeing, hearing and smelling are natural properties of a living physical body. The mystic faculties are closed because our energy is dissipated inefficiently on the material and lower subtle levels. Mystic ability is natural but we deprive ourselves by overdosing on social interests.

The use of the brow chakra and the crown chakra cannot be had so long as the life force is occupied processing excessive food intake, excessive stools, excessive sexual interest and general laziness in spiritual pursuits. Only when the life force is freed from these excessive duties, will it naturally rise up the spine and penetrate the brain to activate the brow and crown chakras.

Life force Penetrates Brain

Intellectual Enlightenment

Theoretical spiritual advancement and practical spiritual experience are separate aspects. All the religious doctrines are first accepted through the hearing sense. They all stress hearing as most essential, but hearing is just the start. After hearing one should take up disciplines and experience definite results. Attraction of the divine grace and reception of it clears the way for spiritual experience through which the doctrine becomes practical.

Without spiritual experience, spiritual life is a theoretical achievement only and is not soul-felt. One must be very careful in selecting a spiritual path since if one joins a society which promises spiritual experience, one may in fact never experience any of it, despite years of following the process.

The divine grace is there but unless one becomes disciplined, the grace usually does not descend into one's being, so one does not get the required experiences and is instead, left with a belief only, thus reducing religion to a system of faith in a particular doctrine and a hope that at the time of death, everything will change drastically for the better.

A religion must give the result of character reformation or the removal of destructive vices and bad behavior. If it cannot do that, it is either useless or the follower is not adhering to the process. Many people remain in a religious society and never take up the disciplines completely but they pretend to be loyal to the system. At the same time, some religions make false promises which the adherents will never achieve.

Apart from character reformation, a religious system should provide religious experience of higher states; otherwise it is merely a belief system, thriving on the superstitious tendency of human beings. By experience of higher states, one's confidence in the religion improves in real terms, since promises made about the hereafter are felt, seen, touched and sensed.

Apart from character reformation and higher states, a religion must also give experience of higher bodies beginning with the subtle body. It just cannot be merely a belief in higher bodies. For instance, in some Western religions, people do not believe in a subtle body at all. They believe there is no subtle body and that at the time of death they will all of a sudden assume an angelic form and be transported into the presence of God. But such a system of belief is insufficient for an effective religious system. If it is true that they will be transported, they should get some experience beforehand. If there is no prior experience, their idea of themselves as a material body will continue at the time of death and even if they were transported they will soon return to this earthly place by the momentum of the human tendency. Religion should give total experience and the follower must see to it that he follows the religion sincerely, taking up all the disciplines in order to know how much the religion actually yields.

Of course every follower does not have the required enthusiasm but those who do, the more sincere people, should make full endeavor and test the system. There is no point in spending many years following a religion only to find out at death that it does not give the promised result, either because parts of it were imaginary or because we did not take up the disciplines sufficiently. Let us test it now so that we can make the necessary adjustments before passing from the body.

If we are making a mistake in the way we follow, let us find out now so that we can adjust and also advise others who are blindly following. If the religion or method makes false promises, let us discover the misrepresentation.

Meditation

Perhaps the most disturbing aspect of meditation is irritating thoughts which come from acquaintances whose minds are not under control and who seek to relate to the meditator by thought transference. In part, this harassment by thought communication is done unconsciously but the effects are devastating. In the *Patañjali Yoga Sūtras* we get a hint in the second *sūtra*:

- *The skill of yoga is demonstrated by the conscious non-operation of the vibrational modes of the mento-emotional energy. (Yoga Sūtras,1.2)*

Of course, no one can show us consciousness as a material object but to *Patañjali,* consciousness was perceptible. He defines yoga as checking the impulsive actions or vibrational modes within consciousness.

Thought control is absolutely essential in the higher stages of any spiritual discipline. From thought, comes activity. Therefore if thoughts are not controlled, actions cannot be controlled. Controlling thoughts means discerning which ideas in the mind are one's own and which enter from outside sources. One must also discern which of these are of spiritual interest and which are truly detrimental to spiritual aims.

Once an idea enters the mind one has to discern the origin and worth of it, rather than deal with the idea and then find out the consequences. Usually we deal with all mental ideas by embracing them if they seem agreeable or discarding them if they seem disagreeable. For meditation one should use a different assessment in terms of the spiritual worth of an idea regardless of its immediate pleasure or pain-giving value.

In the higher stages one first checks the idea and then one assesses it quickly or gradually instead of reacting by rejection or acceptance. The process is one of instant or gradual thorough assessment just after the idea is detected in the mind. The first part of assessment is determining the source of the idea. Is it the thinker's idea? Is it an idea that entered the mind and surfaced in the consciousness in the form of a mental sound, picture or feeling?

Usually one assumes that any thought or image was created by the self in the mind. Many ideas that I experience within the mind are not my own, nor can I stop every idea from others from entering my mind. I can greatly limit ideas from outside by limiting my association with others but I cannot stop it completely because the interaction of thoughts and mental vibrations between individuals is a natural process. It is a law of nature that one cannot keep the mind totally isolated. One can only limit idea entry by limiting association through purification of the emotions.

First one must discover an outside idea without acting on it or reacting to it impulsively. Then one must determine whose idea it is. Once one determines this, one must consider the worth of the suggestion. If it is degrading, one should reject it in a way whereby one decreases the associations that produced or encouraged the idea. It is not a matter of rejecting all foreign ideas because some come from superior beings who have one's spiritual interest at heart and by whose grace one can progress further. Thus it is a process of finding the worth of the idea and recognizing the progressive or non-progressive source.

A bad idea that arose from one's own nature must be handled carefully to determine why one's nature produced it. If one analyzes this, one can cure the self of faulty habits. If the idea is bad, and if it is from outside the psyche, one can carefully, in thought, word and deed, take steps to avoid the person who produced it.

One cannot progress in spiritual life just by one's own good or spiritually-worthy views. One must take help from others and should learn to welcome ideas from the divine beings or elevated masters who might influence one with good conceptions and good motivations in spiritual life. Bad ideas from lowly beings or even from seekers of a comparable level of advancement, should be carefully screened without being processed mentally. Once one recognizes a destructive foreign idea, one should express a holding power over it, so that it stays at a distance, where it can be assessed with less contamination. If it is detrimental to spiritual life, one should just leave it where it is in the mind, without bringing it closer to the core-self. One should handle it in such a way as to starve it of attention. If one does this, it will fade away.

In the mature stage of thought control, one is able to let an idea be, without becoming personally involved or one may reject a bad idea, but in the case of rejection there is a form of energy that feeds the idea and causes subsequent reactions of mental energy in the mind, as well as social reactions with persons on the external plane later. In the advanced stage one avoids all this internal and external turmoil by giving the idea no attention. As soon as it is sufficiently starved, the idea fades away.

Spiritually-destructive thoughts can come from dependents and be projected into the mind of a teacher. They can come from fellow seekers. It is even possible for a teacher to send counterproductive thoughts to a disciple. Therefore everyone, the master and the less advanced seekers, must protect the self by carefully checking all ideas which surface in the mind. It is not that one cannot trust anyone, for it is not possible to exist in this world without trusting others. Trust is required but we should discriminate and assess the thoughts and energies which come to us.

Once one gets to the level where one can instantly analyze an idea and deal with it to disintegrate or develop it, one simultaneously develops the ability to eliminate lower qualities. When we recognize low thoughts in the mental space, we understand the parts of our nature that are impure. We work internally to change that condition. This process occurs deep within the conscious and subconscious mind to rid us of undesirable impressions from past lives. It helps us to anchor and establish divine associations within the mind. In our present condition the superconscious is not accessible. We are stuck with contaminated mental energy which we tried to sanctify in so many ways. However when the inner nature is purified we begin to feel superconsciousness and to function consciously through and in it. This prepares the way for development or realization of a spiritual body.

Impurities in human nature serve a purpose to keep the living being anchored in a certain level of consciousness where he can function objectively and not be spaced out. The impurities do have a positive function in that way but the disadvantage is that they bar one from adopting anything higher than the materialistic view. Thus it is necessary for the evolved entities to be purified from lower qualities and to attain a higher, more pure conception of themselves and of life.

Chapter 11

Meditation is Required

A formal system of meditation is a necessity even in these trying times when we hardly have leisure. Lack of meditation results in insanity, disorderliness and impracticality. Despite the unfavorableness of the times, despite the fact that we have little recreation, meditation still remains a necessity. A man who has gone totally insane may avoid meditation, but any person with a bit of sense does some meditation either consciously or unconsciously. Our emotions, thinking apparatus and material body cannot function properly without mental relaxation. Haphazard meditation does give results. This is how many of us meditate. We are involved in a skip-and-hop, sporadic, impulsively-motivated mental relaxation. Meditation, like sleep, cannot be avoided.

I recommend some type of formal meditation on a daily basis for a minimum of fifteen minutes to begin with. In addition to these fifteen minutes, each person should try to simmer down before resting and should reconsider their life for about thirty minutes before drifting to sleep each evening.

Simmering down is preparation for meditation. It is not meditation itself. Simmering down is sufficient to keep most of us in a state of sanity. Simmering down quiets the mental and emotional activities. It protects us from near-total exhaustion on the psychic level, the place from where insanity develops and spreads.

Too much responsibility brings on madness. Too little responsibility brings on carelessness, which is a type of madness. Clumsiness in dealing with our assigned responsibilities brings unrest which is a stage leading to madness.

In the preliminary stages, meditation means being quiet for a while. But when one tries to be quiet one discovers many factors about the psyche and the external environment. Even if the environment could be quieted, our nature would buzz. Silence or silent meditation brings us to the realization that everything is active. In terms of vibration, everything is moving. Nothing is absolutely still. I can go into the darkest forest on the darkest night, far, far away from any human habitation and I will hear a noise. There will be vibration. It cannot be eliminated. This is the first realization in trying to meditate. There is no such thing as a completely quiet environment. The whole creation is buzzing with vibrations on every level.

We need not search for absolute silence but we need to find wholesome vibrations, which reinforce the essential being. We should look for an environment that reinforces the core-self, not one that entices, misuses and confuses it. In trying to meditate over and over, one will, of necessity, learn some of these truths.

The advice is: Do not search for a quiet place to meditate. Instead, locate the most conducive environment. Be practical with yourself and with nature. Do not feel that you must find the very best place. Providence may not agree that you deserve the very best. Make use of the best that is presented to you by circumstance. Find that most conducive place. Meditate there. Until your location and situation change for the better, be satisfied where you are.

When, in this present body, I first became serious about deliberate meditation, it was the year of 1970. By that time, I had done quite a bit of meditation, but I was not serious about it. Unfortunately, destiny did not agree that I should be in a very quiet place at the time. Periodically, destiny used to release me and allow me to go to an isolated beach. I would look at wide, panoramic Pacific sunsets off Blue Beach on the island of Luzon in the Philippines. I wanted absolute silence. If I could find such a place, I reasoned, I would be free from distractions and could discover whatever there was deep within my nature. On that isolated beach, I observed that even though there were no human beings in the vicinity, there were insects making trillions of tiny noises. Even though there were no man-made lights, there were an unlimited number of microscopic, floating sea creatures glowing in the darkness. The ocean roared constantly. Realizing that the search for complete silence was futile, I was resigned to reality.

The meaning is: When we first set out to meditate, we do so with a distorted sense of purpose. We feel that we deserve total peace. Eventually we realize that as impossible. Later I gave up attachment to finding an absolutely quiet place. I decided in all humility that I should accept whatever environment destiny would allow. We only deserve the best facility which destiny affords us and nothing better until destiny finds it convenient to relieve us.

The author had a small room in a military barracks. By the grace of destiny, there was a closet. I went into that cramped space, closed the door, considered and meditated. I began to realize that I was not the center of life. Life was not meant for my satisfaction. In fact, I was meant to satisfy life. In the search for something convenient, I discovered that I was to be a convenience for life. In trying to centralize myself, I discovered that life intended to keep me on the periphery.

I started meditation with the idea that I should be free from distractions and that I was entitled to be free of everything unpleasant. I soon realized that such a desire was madness. It was a misunderstanding. After this, I became very, very happy to meditate anywhere. I was content to find the best part of any situation and make the best use of it, being humble towards providence.

I learned to regulate meditation around social duties. I could not meditate when I wanted to. I was required to be at a place of employment at certain times. I coordinated meditation around that schedule. I did not give up employment for the sake of meditation but kept the job and meditated in spare time.

If nature is full of vibrations, what about the inner being? Can we find absolute quiet there? The answer is yes and no. In the beginning of meditation, we will not find any absolute or near-absolute peace and quiet there. To expect that, all of a sudden, we will find internal silence or order is to expect too much of ourselves. We have many stored mental impressions. We have a jumble of vibrations. We should not be angered or disappointed by this. We should smile with ourselves and consider how foolish we were, for having taken in so many incompatible vibrations.

We must wrestle with unfavorable impressions for months or years, depending on how contaminated we are. If we looked at visual media, we would have millions of impressions. To remove these would take time and persistent practice.

We will have to practice mental concentration of the mind before mastering meditation. In such concentration, bad impressions will surface. We should inspect them and develop methods of removing their energy from the psyche. Concentration on a mantra, on a deity, on an internal point, on internal light, on the core-self or on the Supreme Self, is like a gate through which these unwanted impressions are pushed out of the psyche. But while some imprints leave and never re-enter, others have a recurring power through which they leave and re-enter repeatedly. We may learn from a competent teacher how to deal with these persistent impressions.

What started as an attempt at meditation, is reduced to being an attempt at removing unwanted impressions. Unless these are removed, deep meditation cannot be attained.

Sometimes mental disturbances quiet down all by themselves. Then we are freed to consider in clarity, to rest and exist in peace. Still, this does not last. While there is some mental peace, we may discover that there is no absolute silence. There is constant inner vibration, be it favorable or unfavorable.

Mind Management in Terms of Music

In the beginning meditation does not mean meditation. It means mind management. This means to concentrate and learn how to manage the mental and emotional energy. This is not meditation, but if mastered this serves as a basis for meditation.

For mind management one should give up the addiction to music. One should regulate music intake and be very selective in the type of music heard. As modern people with electronic means, we are overly attached to media. Presently there is more music being produced than ever before. Meditation as it is defined in the *Yoga Sūtras* means stopping all unfavorable mental impressions. It implies cleaning the mind of the bad impressions that lie within it. Generally speaking, radios and televisions are against any type of meditation practice. The study of why we become addicted to music is an important consideration. Unless we understand clearly the need for music, we will not be able to curb our attachment to it.

Music is a form of sensual gratification. It can be a form of intoxication. It brings happiness. It banishes problems and eases tensions. It foreshadows reality. It helps us to avoid dealing with inadequacies. Music is very valuable as an escape from inconvenient realities. We need to curb the intake of it if we intend to clean the mind. Through music, many unwanted impressions enter the mind.

Insofar as these obstruct meditation, we should give up the addiction and limit the intake, carefully screening the type we hear. Instead of banishing sorrow with music, we might try tracing the cause of the sorrow and deal with that. Or we might try facing the cause of the depression and anxiety and honestly work to eliminate that.

When music is taken into the mind it may recur in the mind at any time. This applies to any type of music, whether it is desirable or undesirable. Even religious music can become a vice. Even that can recur in the mind as a humbug distraction.

The mind is sensitive. Its sensitivity may pose a problem if we want to meditate. We should learn to guard the mind from various stimuli, from various energies that enter it and cause it to become impulsive.

Random Thought

A big problem for meditators is random thought. This must be curbed. First of all, one should learn to protect the mind from unnecessary impressions. The mind is very sensitive and very susceptible to impressions which come through the five senses. The mind is also affected by the psychic world. The psychic senses allow the mind to pick up sounds that cannot be heard physically. The mind can see things that cannot be seen physically. It can touch things that cannot be touched physically. It can taste and smell psychically. Someone might be in America. Someone might be in India. The mind is so sensitive that it can detect thoughts of someone located thousands of miles away. The mind may absorb an idea from someone else's thought patterns and process that energy haphazardly.

When the mind absorbs a thought, it pursues that idea. If allowed, it processes the concept to a conclusion. The mind will go on processing one thought after another continuously. It uses much psychic energy to handle and convert thoughts. When a person sits to meditate, he or she may observe this mental sequence. The person may struggle to control the mind. In struggling one may discover that one does not have the power to stop this. Does this happen only when one sits to meditate?

It happens at all times but when one meditates one notices it. Usually one is too distracted to analyze the mind's activities. In meditation, one observes this. As one struggles and struggles, one might give up on mind control. Many people avoid meditation as a path of spiritual life because they had the experience of not being able to control the mind. They conclude that direct mind control is impossible. Instead of wasting time in a hopeless battle with the mind they assume indirect methods of mind subjugation. One such method is to ignore the mind. In others, one engages the mind in an activity or sound. These alternate methods may or may not work. If a method works, meditation becomes possible.

The mind has a way where it misleads the meditator into doing everything good except the good thing that is desired. It avoids directed, self-focused action. Since the soul might be irritated if the mind creates a bad thought, the mind may react by creating good thoughts. These are distractions nevertheless. The soul should learn to stop the mind from pursuing any undesired thought. Unless the mind gets energy from the soul it cannot pursue its objectives. Thus we should observe how the mind acquires and utilizes energy. We should regulate the meeting point between the mind and the soul. These aspects of spiritual life cannot be attained without deep study of meditation manuals like Bhagavad-Gītā as well as by discussions with great souls who have faced these bad habits and have curbed the mind satisfactorily.

For success, a certain amount of deliberate effort is required. By association with an advanced meditator one will get some advancement free of charge, but that progress will vaporize if one does not practice the disciplines. Certain aspects of spiritual life are developed by individual effort alone. In some areas the teacher can advise and set an example, but the student must eventually assume the practice himself.

Mind Support

The mind needs a certain amount of support from the soul. The soul is linked to the mind by a sense of deliberation. This sense of deliberation is usually called the intellect or *buddhi*. The soul is not directly linked to the general mind stuff except through the sense of deliberation.

By psychology a human being intensifies mystic activities when he is physically restricted. If an individual is barred from visiting a loved one, he will visit the person with more intensity on the mental and dream planes. He will go to that person in the subtle body more regularly in dreams.

The mind has many layers. While I am following good advice, the mind usually shifts to another level and enacts contrary thoughts. Unless I find a method to confront the mind, I will not be able to stop bad association on subtle levels. Suppose I have spiritually productive energy, what will stop my mind from thinking of worldly associations on other levels? What will stop my subtle body from finding worldly association during sleep when it separates from the gross body?

We should realize the undesirable habits of the mind, whereby the mind shifts to other levels and continues unwanted habits, even when we practice spiritual disciplines. We should find a discipline that corners the mind and restrains it totally. It is a matter of honestly realizing that we are manipulated by the mind. A process of mind control is ineffective if we discover that while practicing, the mind continues to act impulsively on other levels.

The intellect is like an engineer, a planner, but it will not lift a finger to manhandle the mind unless the soul directs it to do so. If the soul wants everything to work smoothly, automatically, without a certain amount of direction, then the soul will remain as a pawn in the mind. Things will work smoothly but in the material way only, not for spiritual advancement.

When the mind gets information it may or may not retain it. In either case, it cannot hold any information forever. The mind will of necessity, have to release a portion of any information. When the information is released it goes to a deeper layer as a stored impression. This deeper layer is called the subconscious. To help the soul, it would be required that in some instances, the body takes notes or puts information in written form before all facts slip from the functional mind into the subconscious.

Social Problems

Even in spiritual life, even in isolation, there are daily social problems. There are problems of climate and food. These are the most basic problems which cause us to interact with each other outside of spiritual life. Even if one goes to an ashram, he will have to take shelter from the weather. He will have to acquire eatables. He will have to interact to some degree. We should try our utmost to decrease this interaction. This means a great reduction in the desire to exploit gross and subtle matter. But such reduction should be implemented through purification of the psyche. Religions that focus on our external conditions hardly help us to reduce desires. These religions inflate our needs while trying to sanctify and pass them off as something divine.

The weather is controlled by supernatural energy and the overall pattern of it has to do with the overall favorable and unfavorable reactions that are due to humanity. The weather will of necessity, be adverse from time to time. There is a need for shelter or lodging. Some saintly people do become immune to adverse weather conditions but they do so only after much austerity and hardening of their mental profile towards emotions. Others, who are not so detached, must do something to deal with the weather. This is done by building dormitories, ashrams, guest houses and the like; but one must acquire assistance for this, either by getting free labor from other human beings or by acquiring money to employ them. In either case one must interact socially. Such interaction poses a danger of exploiting people unfairly. Many a spiritual movement or spiritual life of an ascetic is ruined by awkward dealings with the public or by exploiting the public through tricks in order to induce people to give help or money.

Food must be acquired. This means one must either farm himself or get produce from others. If one farms, he requires land and a means of tilling it. He requires seeds or seedlings. He requires food storage facilities. He may have to protect produce from frost or excessive heat. If he cannot grow everything, he will have to trade or acquire money. In some cases on a plea of being saintly, an ascetic induces others to give food. Material nature does pressure the aspiring seeker to cheat. In that way nature creates a basis for the ruination of his character. To get out of this cheating, one should reduce one's needs.

As social problems arise, one should solve them on the spot. If one allows problems to pile up into a backlog of unfinished tasks, one's spiritual life will be affected. First, one should simplify as much as possible by cutting out excessive desires. Let us take for example, the seeker who lives in a very large house. He may conclude that the expense of such a large house hampers spiritual life. Thus he may get a smaller residence. But even then, there might be problems. During the rainy season, the roof might leak. Therefore, as soon as possible, the leak should be repaired. The seeker should not live from day to day with a leaky roof and damp house on his mind. It is better to fix the roof and be done with it. Of course in material nature, there is a need for endless maintenance because matter is endlessly changing. Still, the seeker should not be lazy but should be energetic and efficient in maintaining the surroundings. At the same time, he should also keep his life as simple as possible.

Some people try to exploit the austerities of a saintly man by offering assistance for shelter and food but a saintly man should not sell himself to others just for food and lodging. Even a saintly man should be willing and able to work honestly to acquire his needs. If one allows others to exploit oneself, one will regret it. There are many human beings who have an expertise of exploiting the austerities of a saintly man. They offer him a room, a meal or some convenience and they keep him like a caged animal.

Problems which are not solved, remain in the mind to affect one's meditation. It is in one's interest to solve these on a daily basis so that they do not have a continuous and aggregate negative influence. Procrastination or the habit of delaying in the performance of duties and routine tasks, is harmful to one's spiritual life. There were great sages who neglected their duties and routine tasks and were successful in spiritual life but these persons were performing certain strict austerities through which they were excused by the divine grace. One cannot get such exemption if one is not performing hard-core austerities. One should be up and about to complete duties and routine tasks as efficiently as possible.

Psychic Blindness

Psychic eyes do exist but for the time being they are closed, just as the eyes of newborn kittens are sealed. If there were no eyes in the subtle body, we could not see through physical eyes. If the subtle body has no importance, then our material body has even less meaning and significance. However it is to the contrary; the subtle body is important. The mind is the brain of the subtle form. The emotions of this body, which reside mostly in the chest region, come from the chest of the subtle form. As the eyes in the head are protrusions and functions of the physical brain, so the subtle eyes are extensions of the subtle mind.

Negative Mind Content

Regardless of the type of method used, one should deal with negative mind contents. This means that if we take in a destructive idea, we should promptly eliminate it. A person chanting, for instance, will find that while chanting, the mind creates images and other types of mind constructions that disrupt the focus. The same experience comes while meditating, considering or concentrating. While chanting, one may avoid this negative mind content but while meditating, one has to face it. In meditation there is nothing to cover distractions. With chanting one can briefly avoid or try to escape by focusing on the sound. While meditating one has to face it squarely.

Meditation therefore serves to alert a seeker to his bad ideas. He sees exactly what he allowed into his mind. Meditation can be frustrating in a way and very revealing in another. What we can run from repeatedly while chanting, we have to face in meditation, to see what violence we did to ourselves by allowing certain impressions to enter. As long as we are not as absorbed externally, the mind begins to act more on the internal plane. It works and re-works stored information and ideas. Then we perceive internally what was absorbed by the mind.

In meditation one should clear out the undesirable aspects. After trying to meditate with clarity and trying for minutes or hours, one realizes that one must clear off the bad energy. It is better therefore to first clear the bad ideas and then meditate, making this the routine of meditation. Instead of wasting time trying to meditate at first, begin your meditation by dismissing the trashy mental ideas. When these are removed, meditation may be conducted.

Management and Elimination of Exploitive Tendencies

The tendency to exploit others is very strong in human existence. All phases of spiritual development are affected by the tendency to use others. Material nature presents opportunities for this usage continuously. If we do not resist it, we will be implicated in exploitive acts. One must live very simply with a few needs and keep one's planning impulse under control, or else one will be carried away by impractical planning. After such planning when one finds that the world is not responding as desired, one will invent schemes which will cause a backlash.

It is seen that even some great spiritual masters cannot resist the tendency to exploit others. They proceed with it confidently and ruin their reputations in the process. In some cases, when we meet someone for the first time, we inquire of his skill, finances, and relations. Then we begin to plan how to use him. All of this is a sort of parasitic view of life. It is detrimental to our spiritual progress and turns a good friendship sour in the long run.

One may meet someone, hear of his skills, motivations, finances and relationships and then keep such information filed in the mind until one figures a way to use him. All such questioning, figuring, filing and usage are against spiritual advancement.

Character Reformation

Reformation of one's character is a long, drawn-out process. It does not happen overnight even if one uses the most powerful method. After we take up a spiritual practice, bad tendencies may sink deep into the subconscious. As soon as the initial phase passes, these tendencies surface in the conscious decision-making mind and assert with great force. One by one, we should observe the bad tendencies, work on them, observe their exhibition, resist them, replace them with preferred traits, and then eradicate them completely by simplifying our lives and giving up lust, greed and offensive anger. It takes time. We should not assume that we are so pure that we cannot be purified further.

Isolation

Isolation has value but it is not everything. A living entity has a time for isolation and a time for social mixing. One must learn how to remain isolated some of the time. As soon as one goes into isolation, one will be attacked on the mystic plane with greater force. One will have to face up to shortcomings, loneliness, and the need to be with others. Isolation shows the psychic side of life and gives us an understanding of how we are affected by it. It reveals subconscious impressions which come up repeatedly to unsettle and draw us back to the material world.

In isolation, dreams are more intense and psychic association is clearer. We begin to see that we have problems on the physical as well as on the psychic side. Isolation may teach one to curtail physical acts and to carefully regulate physical associations. As long as we are focused on the gross material side, we will fail to understand what sort of violence we do to ourselves by careless association with others.

The subtle body is durable and lasting; the gross form will be scrapped sooner or later. These two are quite separate. The interaction of the two must be observed if we are to be freed from the bodily concept of life. The influence of a body on the soul cannot be overstated, for the soul is affected when it has a body and also when it loses one. When we have a material body, our tendency is to act as if we are identical with that form. When we lose a material body, we usually crave a new one. This craving for a new body is present even when we possess a living one. Many of our social relationships are based on our anticipated future need for a new human form.

For instance, since this writer is a poor man, he might cultivate friendships with wealthy persons with an underlying motive of eventually getting his next body in a wealthy family. His discontent with poverty might well drive him to desire a transfer to a wealthy family at the time of death.

Since the author does not have a university education, he might try to make friends with educated people, so that in his next life he could write books bearing all the credentials that are accepted in educated circles. In this way, he will still be motivated from the material level. He may practice internal dishonesty by telling himself that he associates with wealthy persons to encourage them in spiritual life.

These negative aspects all have to do with the influence of the body on the soul and the soul's inability to use the body for spiritual gain. Eating is related, because the body lives on air and food. These two ingredients are even more essential than money and education.

For spiritual life, a reduction of food intake will be necessary. If one is serious about meditation, he will have to cut back on the mass of food and closely regulate the time of eating. Much of the food we eat can be substituted by increased oxygen intake and increased meditative rest. Meditative rest frees the mind from anxieties. It rejuvenates the mind and body.

Much haphazard thinking is related to bad diet and insufficient rest. We may eat to our heart's content but if we do not rest sufficiently, the mind and brain will be erratic. Our plans will become more and more impractical and implicating in material nature.

One or two short naps during the day are necessary for sanity. These naps should be for the most, one hour, and for the least, fifteen minutes. These should be of a meditative and contemplative nature so the mind remains awake but is freed from anxieties and worries. In meditation, the mind should be cleaned of accumulated trashy thoughts and checked closely for unfavorable emotions. If found, these should be promptly removed.

During such resting periods, one should learn how to keep the mind away from the frontal regions of the brain where it easily and impulsively engages in ongoing, uncontrolled thinking.

One should deliberately move the mind upwards or to the back of the head, where the mind stops its undesirable thinking and picturization habits. One should also try to connect himself to advanced meditators so as to free the mind from association with ordinary folks.

Normally the mind focuses through the facial area of the head. This area gives the core-self little cooperation in its effort to control the mental functions. I suggest that beginners refrain from confining the mind in this area and instead move the attention of the core-self to the back area of head.

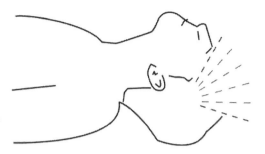

The core-self must become convince that when it focuses through or into the facial area of the mind, it has the least control over mental functions.

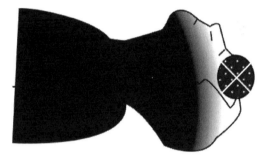

Practice moving the mental energy backwards around the head.

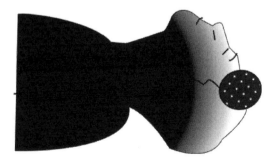

Keep moving the mental energy backwards around the head

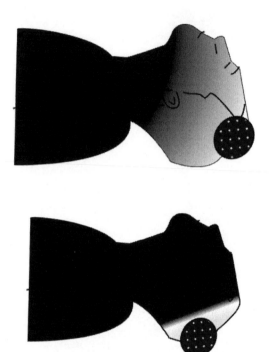

Move the mental energy to the lower back area of the head. Hold that energy in this location. If the energy disappears, it means that it has resumed its normal position in the facial area. Return your attention to that area and begin the practice again. Be patient.

Instructions

Eat less. Learn *prāṇāyāma* and breathe more.

Consider air as part of your diet, by learning how to draw more air into the lungs. Learn to see air as a form of nourishment.

Eat less. Rest more. Replace some meals by a rest break.

For example, during a lunch break one may rest the mind quietly and remove its anxieties.

Astral Freedom

At the time of death even a person who does not believe in psychic power and who spent a lifetime denying it, will have to face it. At that time all such denial will come to an abrupt end, because one will no longer have a material body to hide in. It is best to cultivate some awareness of the subtle body now. Even if one believes that he will get spiritual salvation in heaven, paradise, or the kingdom of God, one has nothing to lose by cultivating awareness of the subtle form.

If we are afraid of the subtle body, of its discovery, then how will we face it at the time of death? The legendary spiritual body is even more flimsy than the subtle one. If we are attached to this flesh-and-blood existence and deny the psychic side, it is quite unreasonable to assume that we will acquire a spiritual body at the time of death.

Just before sleeping in the evening, one may lie in a firm bed on the back and practice freeing the subtle body. This can be done as a regular practice for at least fifteen minutes. For that little time, one can free the self from the material conception of life. As the body lies on the back, we can imagine the subtle body assuming various anti-gravity positions. One quality of the subtle form that distinguishes it from the gross one, is its ability to defy gravity, to move up or down through the air or even through solid materials. Just as radio waves penetrate buildings, the subtle body transcends solid matter. The subtle form, like a radio wave, has higher frequencies. As a radio wave is made up of subtle electrical energy and is transmitted with piercing power, so the subtle body is made up of higher vibrational energy.

Here are some diagrams to show how to imagine some anti-gravity positions. The word "imagine" means more than just speculation. As a merchant may plan or imagine the purchase of wholesale goods on the next business day, so you would imagine the subtle body's separation as shown. One begins this practice by imagining. After some practice, the subtle body may respond and do exactly as conceived.

Awareness of physical body lying down

Awareness of astral and physical body lying down

The astral body is merely the psychology or psychic make-up of the personality. This is also called the psyche. It is depicted in these diagrams as the dark figure. The physical body is the outlined white figure. The mental and emotional energy make up the psyche and this forms the subtle body which is experienced in dreams. When the gross body dies, one discovers that one's identity is this subtle body, just as when one is born in this world through a mother, one realizes oneself as a baby form which grows into adulthood.

Astral body floating at the side of the gross form

The astral body is not subjected to the same gravitational force which keeps the gross body attached to the earth. The astral form floats. There is a gravitational pull on it but it is a psychological one which is based on the attachments of the person to the material world. In the following diagram the astral body turned over and is facing downward. It can pass through the earth or any other solid object because it's made of subtle energy.

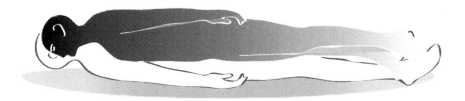

Astral Body floating upside down

The astral body can float upside down but usually it does this on its own. Initially an astral projector is unable to control the upward, downward or sideways movement of the astral form. However by constant practice, one gains control.

If one finds oneself in the astral body and it is upside down, one should not panic. Anxiety may cause one to be immediately drawn back into the gross body, thus abruptly ending the experience. If fear or excitement arises in the astral body, that energy may cause it to be fused back into the gross form.

Astral body floating upside down facing backwards

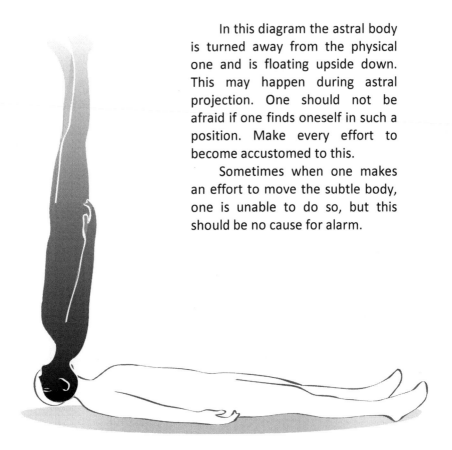

In this diagram the astral body is turned away from the physical one and is floating upside down. This may happen during astral projection. One should not be afraid if one finds oneself in such a position. Make every effort to become accustomed to this.

Sometimes when one makes an effort to move the subtle body, one is unable to do so, but this should be no cause for alarm.

Astral body interspaced into the earth

The astral body unlike the physical one can be interspaced into any solid material. It may enter the earth or pass through concrete. If this happens one should not be afraid of it. Sometimes, however, while in the astral body, one maintains the physical perspective and when the subtle body approaches a solid structure, one becomes afraid of colliding with it. By contant practice one develops the required astral objectivity, and is able to differentiate between its abilities and those of the physical form.

Astral body near the feet of the physical form, facing away from the physical form

Even though the astral body may appear to be standing on the earth or on any solid surface, it cannot do so as a physical form can. It can only float in that position. It can however express a gravitational attitude when it is in a dimension which has the same vibrational consistency as itself. In fact when the astral body is in such a world, everything seems solid in reference to it.

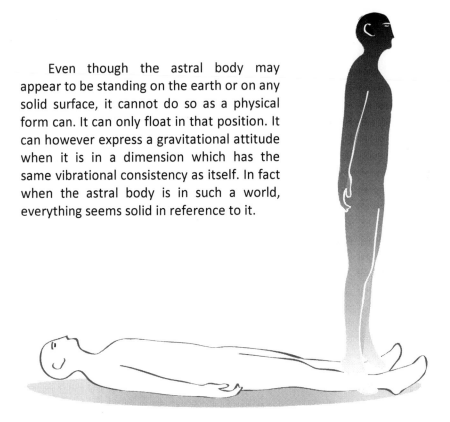

In these diagrams, the imagination will trigger actual experiences. Later, as the gross body sleeps, the mind may become aware of the subtle form. The subtle body usually tries to complete preconceived ideas. If such views are practical for the subtle body, it will automatically duplicate these.

Whatever we think of that we cannot complete physically, may be executed by the subtle form while the gross body sleeps, except that usually we do not recall what the subtle form did. This lack of recall is traceable to an impulsive focus on the physical side. We avoid the psychic side because we are more attached to solid materials. In other words, we are materialistic. At the time of death, we will have to deal with the psychic side, at least until we acquire another baby form, or until we go to Paradise.

Parallel Worlds

There are parallel gross worlds, just as gross as this physical one that we inhabit. These worlds are not visible to our telescopes or physical eyes but they exist. At the time of death some of these worlds will, all of a sudden, become visible to us. In fact, at death, we might all of a sudden be transferred to one of these places.

In one astral experience, I causelessly, without desiring it, entered such a world. Everything was set up in a similar way to this earthly place but I did not recognize any similar religious beliefs there. However when I entered, I used a similar physical body to the one used here. I did not look much different from the local inhabitants. A permanent resident of that other world offered a house for a reasonable rental.

Admittedly, at the time of the experience, I forgot about my existence on this planet. This particular forgetfulness is something we need to understand before the time of death. All of a sudden at the time of death, one might be transferred to some other world, and one may forget everything about this existence and never recall anything of it again. We need to consider this possibility now, since we might have been transferred here from another place and have no recall of the previous location.

In that other world there was no radio or television. Such gadgets were not invented. The soil was fertile. The vegetation and flowers were different. There were no crowded living conditions, no slum areas and no cities like New York where millions of people live in skyscrapers.

They had bicycles and primitive slow-moving cars. They spoke a language which had a grammatical layout very similar to English. The body I assumed automatically translated my thoughts into that language. A man offered a place to rent. I found that I had sufficient money, so I took the place. When a neighbor lady observed that I moved in, she locked her gates. She sensed that I was different. She was overcome with fear.

After this I went into the house. Soon after, I found myself in this world again. Upon returning, my Krishna Deity said, "I showed you this to provide evidence of other unexploited planets. The earth is ecologically ruined. Be assured of other untouched places."

To escape the gross, one must take shelter in the subtle. This is what the celestial beings do on a permanent basis. They remain anchored in the subtle celestial world. To escape the subtle body, one must become sheltered in the causal form. This is what some great yogis do. They do not take rebirth during a time cycle which lasts for millions of years. Sometimes they come as saviors. Then they return to the causal plane and hide from the cries of the lower beings. On the causal plane, one must be content with mere intentions and motives and that means living as and in enriched mental and emotional energy.

Chapter 12

Mystic Insight

Readers need a notebook, kept by the bedside at night and kept in the pocket during the day. One should record any spiritual experience which forms spiritual ideas, visions, and realization. One should record nighttime experiences which come as dreams, visions, and psychic perceptions. This is important. Many of the subtle experiences which we dismiss as irrelevant are significant in spiritual life. Many of these make no sense until they are reviewed days, weeks or months after. The seeker should take notes and review the notebook from time to time. If we keep notes, some of the experiences will tally with what we heard from authoritative sources. Some of it will form a pattern of spiritual development. From the notes we may separate illusion from valid psychic experience.

Hearing about a foreign country is one thing and actually going there is an entirely different matter, for invariably what we hear is distorted as soon as it enters the mind. Only by travelling to the foreign place can we rectify the distortions. It is worse to hear from someone who heard and who did not experience. When we hear from someone who heard, we subject ourselves to a very faulty process if the hearer did not experience what was heard. The yoga system dictates that a teacher should be experienced.

Someone might wonder, "How can I become a mystic? I am not gifted with supernatural power."

The answer to this can only be given when we correct the self-conception. Mystic insight is personal attention applied to the psychic side of life. It must be applied consistently and habitually. Each person has attention. The problem therefore is how to direct the attention to subtle life. Some are habitually unfocused either on material existence or spiritual life. Of those who are unfocused, some are attached to spiritual life and others to material existence, while others are indifferent to either, not being interested in the material or spiritual side. The common factor here is attention. Each person has attention.

We need to realize our natural condition. What type of person am I? How do I normally use my attention? Attention is mystic insight or to state it more accurately, when attention is consistently and habitually applied to the subtle side, it is called mystic insight. If the attention is applied haphazardly we become disheartened and disappointed, feeling that we are not getting the result. Spiritual life takes time to develop. Usually it is not attained suddenly. If one is impatient one will not develop the mystic side. Someone is a mystic today because he practiced in past lives and has a pattern of mystic focus.

Those who have little or no mystic vision and who desire to have it, may learn from those who cultivated it. We would not acquire it by a method of endowment because by nature, we must cultivate whatever is unnatural. We will have to realize shortcomings and take steps to change gradually over an extended period of time by honest and right endeavor. If for instance, I am habituated to an unfocused life, I will have to use a discipline that can reverse this over a period of time. I will have to apply myself consistently to get results. I should not be impatient. I should not think that I can get success overnight.

The gift of mystic insight comes from application of attention to the psychic side of existence. This means we have to lift our attention from the mundane side, stabilize it and retain it through a method of concentration, and then apply it to the psychic side. When it is first applied, we will get little or no results. Instead we will have to endure in the practice for some time before a result is perceived. If a seed is planted, it does not grow in an instant. It takes time. It will not grow if we dig it up every five minutes in anxiety.

Providence

We will have to be patient and learn how to cooperate with providence even when destiny works against us. Even though we may want to become spiritually successful overnight, providence might object. We will have to realize that providence is greater than ourselves. We will have to study the life pattern, which is designed by providence. We will have to work along with it, while using all spare time to cultivate the spiritual side.

Providence will keep us under its thumb because we are not absolute. It will ease up every now and again, and then we can advance rapidly. We need to be alert to take full opportunity when permitted.

Providence will insist that we take care of mundane responsibilities. We will have to go along with providence, otherwise it will squeeze us. Providence, like a stingy employer, has the upper hand, so we will have to realize that and work along cooperatively, like willing employees who learn how to please a mean supervisor. Still no matter how mean it is, providence will allow us to relax from time to time. And whenever it permits, we should apply ourselves in spiritual life.

Providence will insist that we absorb unfavorable reactions for past actions, regardless of whether we agree or not, regardless of whether the inconveniences make sense or not, and regardless of whether we can remember past activities or not.

Spiritual life cannot be achieved if we repeatedly tangle with providence. It will be checked indefinitely. Providence has more power than we can imagine. We have to strike a balance between the demands of providence and our spiritual needs which are to be met.

Drowsiness is related to time. Time is the arm of providence that grabs us and places us here or there. Efficient utilization of time is essential in spiritual life. Providence has already confiscated so much time. The little that is left should be used for spiritual life. We should use spare time efficiently. Much time is taken for mundane needs. We should conserve and properly utilize time.

Let us take, for instance, the matter of getting a baby form. Even if I get one as soon as I pass from this old body, still I will spend many years in schools, learning basic grammar and mathematics. So much time is utilized just to be educated, learning subjects I forgot from the previous life. Then later I will waste much time realizing the purpose of sexual organs.

So much time will be spent sleeping in ignorance. Sleep is necessary but what about excessive sleep? In fact, what exactly is excessive sleep? How can we tell what is excessive and what is sufficient? One teacher from India said that six hours per day is sufficient. A doctor said that eight hours is sufficient. Who is correct?

Drowsiness

Drowsiness is a concern in meditation practice. Drowsiness, after taking sufficient rest, is a problem in spiritual life. Suppose I take ten hours of sleep and I am still drowsy. What is the cause? I had sufficient sleep but my mind is lackadaisical. I try to stay awake but sleep pulls me into unconsciousness. What is the process of sleep? What pulls me? What force shuts the eyelids? What power makes the brain seem so heavy?

In contrast to drowsiness, there is excessive wakefulness. Sometimes, though I desire sleep, I cannot rest. It is time for sleep but I remain awake. The eyelids do not feel heavy. The brain feels light and easy. The mind thinks. I just cannot fall asleep. Is the same force involved in drowsiness and in excessive wakefulness?

Retraction of Sensual Energy

In the yoga system, retraction of sensual energy is called *pratyāhar*. This *pratyāhar* is neither meditative focus nor absorption. This is a withdrawal through which sensual indulgence ceases temporarily. If we study our nature we may observe that we pass through at least one phase of retraction daily. This phase occurs just before we enter the state of sleep.

Before sleeping one goes through a phase of being forcibly drawn away from the external world. Conversely upon awakening, one finds that one is voluntarily or forcibly pushed out of the chamber of sleep into the world of waking. In the waking world, energy is expended through gross senses. In the world of sleep, it is conserved from gross perception and invested into the dream world where the subtle senses remain activated in varying degrees.

If we want to become mystics, if we want an increase in psychic perception, if we want to get spiritual experiences, we should conserve physical sensual power. So long as there is excessive drainage of energy through the gross senses, we will be unable to focus on the mystic realities.

Pratyāhar means retraction of sensual energy and the discovery of how that energy is distributed and used by various senses. When we feel drowsy, our energies are recalled into the subtle body in a particular way. When drowsy, we lose objectivity and are unable to observe the alteration of consciousness.

Let us take the example of electric power. A radio produces a sound when a switch is closed. As soon as the switch is opened, the radio becomes silent. If we have no knowledge of electric circuits, that is a mystery. If we get some knowledge from a technician, we can begin to understand how the power is withdrawn when the switch is opened.

The deliberate withdrawal of the attention from the senses is *pratyāhar* sensual energy restraint. This is conservation of sensual power. This is preliminary in the meditation process. At the time of sleeping or drowsiness, the attention is withdrawn involuntarily. One should learn how to withdraw it deliberately. First of all, there are many yoga books written on the subject and now science presents theories based on brain research. We should learn how sleep operates, by repeatedly observing how we are pulled through drowsiness.

We sleep each night and still we do not understand the process because as we fall asleep we lose awareness. We lose objectivity. We lose the ability to observe how we are affected. If someone touches you from behind, you cannot see the person unless you turn around or unless the person gives you some indication of his or her identity. When we are moved into sleepiness, it is as if we are being pulled down from behind, gagged, blindfolded, and incapacitated by some force. We are held in such a way that we cannot determine what force affects us. We can learn the process of drowsiness by retracting sensual energy.

Retraction of sensual energy is important in conservation of attentive powers. Unless we pull back the energy, cutting the wastage, we will remain without spiritual experiences.

We must study how we gradually lose consciousness when drowsy. First the energy that surges through the senses is retracted. Then it is cut off completely. Upon awaking, the energies are quickly activated along specific channels to re-energize the senses. How is this done?

A particular sensual organ like the eyeball is like an appliance, like a light bulb. The nerves that lead to that eyeball are like the wires that lead to the light socket. The electric power that surges through the wires is like the attentive power moving out into the eye cells. So, where does the power originate?

Usually a man uses a light bulb without understanding the source of the power that energizes it. He does not know how the power is generated. He is only aware that it is present. He has no control over the stoppage of power. That is controlled by an engineer at the power plant.

Similarly, the power which energizes the senses comes from the life force in the lower part of the body. When this power ceases, we are forced to sleep. How can we realize this life force?

Have you ever noticed how the energy surges to awaken the eyeball, the hearing impulse, the smelling impulse, the touching impulse, and the tasting impulse?

Some force beyond will power operates the bodily senses, but would it be possible for anyone to observe it?

Observation of the Outgoing Tendency

We hardly observe how these bodies are energized. There can be no enjoying tendency in the forms unless they are energized. We are so eager to enjoy and to use these bodies that we do not take the time to study how they are activated. This study is the key to understanding how to retract the sensual energy.

When water is poured into a gutter, the liquid moves in a particular direction, depending on the shape and location of the gutter. The water is like the energy and the gutter is like a particular sense organ such as the eye. Psychological energy flows through the eye in a particular way, depending on the shape of the eye and the cell structure of the optic nerves. This energy can be retracted in a particular way as well. *Pratyāhar*, or retraction and conservation of psychic energies, becomes easy if we understand the particular sense organ we desire to control and if we understand how the energy is infused into that sensing mechanism.

The senses are like wild horses. This is the way that we live in the body, in this body-mind environment. When we are unable to control the senses, they venture in their own way. They carry us along. Sometimes the ride is rough. Sometimes it is smooth. Sometimes it coincides with our desire and sometimes it opposes our wishes. In taming a wild horse one has to use restraint and allowance. Restraint alone will not do because the creature is very powerful. It may kick, jolt, resist, and hurt the trainer.

An expert allows a wild horse to run for a time but then he confines the creature for a time. He does not allow it to wander at all times. One should learn when to indulge a sense and when to restrain it.

One should observe the construction of a particular sense organ; how it is aroused; how much energy makes it impulsive; how much energy makes it manageable; and how much energy puts it into a relaxed state.

The automatic operation of the senses should be curtailed. The good tendencies we desire, only come to us consistently when we establish them and root out the undesirable impulsive ones. This comes by a deliberate effort. When riding a wild horse, the trainer allows the creature to go its own way for awhile. Then he pulls the bridle firmly and steadily and controls the creature for awhile. This process of allowing the horse its way and then controlling it, is repeated again and again, patiently, until the horse is completely curbed from impulsive tendencies and becomes permanently submissive.

We should observe how the energies flow through the various senses and then retract the energy, repeatedly permitting and then retracting, until we get the bodily environment under control. It can be done but it will not happen on a permanent basis by an instant method. Our conditioning in material nature occurred gradually. Our liberation will develop gradually as well. The impetus for liberation comes in an instant, but the actual process of being liberated takes time.

Thinking Energy

Thinking energy should be watched carefully, curbed, changed, and re-fined considerably. When we speak of controlling the senses, we usually mean the outward senses like the eyes, ears, nose, tongue, and the touching sense in the hands. These senses are the offshoots of our needs to see, hear, smell, taste and touch. Control of these senses is one type of sense control. There is another type, that of inner sense control. This is more complicated. In the Bhagavad Gītā, when Arjuna wanted to become an ascetic, Lord Krishna discouraged the attempt. He chided the aspiring ascetics who go to isolated places and think of previous association. In other words, even if we achieve some degree of control over the external senses, we will still have to deal with the internal sense of thinking.

Lord Krishna chided the aspiring ascetics by saying that if they went to an isolated place and kept on thinking of previous gratifications, they were only pretending. If I go into isolation, my psychic association with others will continue on the subtle plane. This is what Krishna indicated to Arjuna. He indirectly warned Arjuna not to leave the battlefield, not to go into isolation, since even in isolation, the hostilities of the enemy soldiers would find him. It would be better for Arjuna to face the situation, than to avoid it and then have to deal with a tremendous amount of psychic energy which would be directed to him in isolation.

For each aspiring transcendentalist it may be different. For instance, a simple-minded, plain person who does not maintain much association may be successful in isolation since such a person would not have a tremendous amount of psychic feedback to contend with. But someone like Arjuna, a famous man, would be in mental turmoil in isolation. He would have no peace as the thoughts of friends and enemies would seek him out ardently.

One may be a very powerful figure in world history, or even in his town or village or even in his family, but he may not be as powerful as a minute thought. Thoughts are so penetrating that even conquerors are subdued by them. Therefore thought control is a special psychic discipline.

We have the problem of the uncontrolled mind. That is one problem and then we have the problem of the uncontrolled minds of others. It is not just a matter of controlling self-made thoughts. We have to deal with thoughts which are created by others. As the sense of hearing is open, due to the design of the ears, so the mind is open to thoughts from any and everywhere. Thus we must control thinking and the susceptibility to the destructive thoughts of others.

I may be regulated in routine mental constructions but sometimes a tiny enticing thought may carry me away. A very tiny thought that is not in my spiritual interest, that may ruin my reputation, may lift me and carry me away. This is worth investigating. How could I stop the influence of such a tiny thought which forces me into dubious involvements and expands my degrading tendencies?

First of all we should recognize foreign thoughts. We have to realize that the mind is so constructed, so designed, that it is always open to reception of foreign thoughts. We should realize that even though the mind is open, there is something we can do to regulate its responses to foreign thoughts.

Rejection of incoming undesirable thoughts is not simply a matter of deciding to reject or ignore such ideas. First of all, a foreign thought cannot be completely banished if we are not completely matured away from the need for the pleasure or excitement which the fulfillment of thought would provide. Let us take the instance of a sex-related thought. If I still desire sexual enjoyment, I would succumb to such a thought even if I took a vow to observe celibacy.

A foreign thought cannot be banished completely unless I understand clearly that there will be resentment for my disregard of such a thought. When a foreign thought is banished, there will be resentment. By banishing such a thought we tactfully reject the person who sent the idea. Such rejection might develop a resentment which may convert into anger in the mind of the person produced the thought.

At a certain stage we learn how to reject thoughts and also dispel the resentment, but the resentment must be dealt with in either a sloppy or efficient way.

Mind Control

Each spiritual discipline involves mind and sense control but some disciplines are involved with mind and sense usage to such a degree that the discipline itself is a danger to the control. In warfare there is death by friendly fire, which means that one soldier intentionally or accidentally kills his countryman. This occurs because the use of weapons is itself a danger to friends and foes alike. Similarly in certain spiritual disciplines there is a danger that one might hurt the self, or an ascetic associate, in the process of trying to advance on the spiritual path.

For instance, there is a practice called tantric yoga, where a husband and wife are trained to make advancement in sex control. Since the discipline involves limited usage of sexual contact, there is a danger that they might become even more involved with sexual energies and lose whatever little advancement they acquired.

In the section of yoga called karma yoga, one is supposed to act in the world with detachment, but that is dangerous since in acting in the world, one cannot in all cases be detached and one might be hurt by a negative reaction from material nature.

Mind Contents

The mind is a compartment and within it are thoughts, feelings, pictures and imaginations. The intellect which is the calculative organ within the mind, is there with its calculations, plans and justifications.

In meditation, one should silence the intellect. If we continue to be entertained by the intellect during meditation, the effort becomes a flop. Then how do we silence it?

Protecting the Mind

Control of the mind involves protection of the mind as well as directly restraining it from undesirable gratifications. In the case of a horse trainer, he must protect the horse from the horse's own memories of its previous wild life. If he fails to do this, the horse may leap out of the fenced area.

Even though a horse can easily leap over a four or five foot fence, the animal will remain behind the wire and actually come to believe that the barrier cannot be crossed. However, if there is a strong impetus, the animal will suddenly realize that it can leap over the fence. If a lion were to enter the field, the horse will all of a sudden discover that a four or five foot fence is no obstacle. This means that the horse trainer must protect the horse from excitement.

In the case of the mind, we must protect the mind from energies that cause anxiety. We must also protect the mind from remembering its former gratifications. As soon as it remembers a vice, it is motivated for indulgence. Mind control is more than mind restraint. Mind control includes mind protection. We should study the various ways in which the mind needs to be protected from its own weaknesses. If you expose the mind to temptations, you may not be able to restrain it.

Bad impressions which are lodged in the mind already, will have to be dealt with by some effective means, but we should not expose the mind any further. We should cease the entry of bad impressions. Then we can stop and cleanse the mind. We must be very strict with the conniving intellect.

A vice is a destructive habit that the mind cannot resist. Therefore the mind should not be exposed to vices. If, for instance, a horse trainer brings a fertile mare in the vicinity, the stallions may become unresponsive to training. The mare represents sexual indulgence and a stallion may not be as cooperative if it senses the female animal. A good trainer keeps stallions in one field out of sight and earshot of mares. We must study the mind and note vices which affect us.

Cleaning the Mind

It is hard enough to clean the mind in preparation for engaging in a sanctified activity. I have noticed repeatedly that as soon as I want to do something beneficial, the mind displays unrelated ideas.

A yogi who passed on recently, Dr. Ramamurti Mishra, told the writer, after he left the material body, that the mind can be cleansed daily of its trashy ideas by opening the gap in the forehead and letting the undesirable energy vent into the open atmosphere.

Opening the Gap in the Forehead

I tried this method and it worked. Before that I spent much time trying to delete undesirable ideas from the mind. I cultivated the habit of programming the mind so that I could do certain things on the subtle level while the gross body rested. This practice took between 15 to 45 minutes to clean the mind. I spent years talking to various yogis and transcendentalists and I could not get an effective method. One teacher told me to chant. I tried that, but I found that the mind dives to other levels where trashy information is stored. During chanting the mind would continually shift to another mental plane and expand undesirable considerations.

Another teacher advised me to focus on the crown chakra. I tried but I found that this method only worked after much concentration, through which the trashy ideas were psychicly burnt as they passed through the chakra.

However, Dr. Mishra's method worked in about 3 minutes. Dr. Mishra said, "If there is no mental cleanliness there is no meditation and no success in whatever discipline of spiritual life one pursues. The mind must be cleaned. It should be so clean that even if you cease the discipline, it still remains in that clean state."

Another yogi, *Śrīla Yogeshwarananda* of Gangotri, who already departed his physical body, gave a method. He gave a method of escape.

According to him no one will be able to clean the mind entirely. He said that when he would return from samādhi trance states, his mind would again resume mundane interest. I asked him if there was any level from which the mind would cease having trashy ideas and he said, "If you are talking about the present mind, which is a mundane instrument, the answer is no. In my experience even when returning from the causal plane, I found that as soon as I would be transferred from that zone, the lower mind would immediately begin putting together trashy ideas. The lower mind is naturally involved with these mundane considerations. Unless it is immobilized by retraction, it will continue the effort for mundane pursuits. You can, however, escape by entering causal space. If you do this, you will notice that the ordinary mind is never transferred with you. And thus you will be free from its influence and association for as long as you remain there."

I asked the same yogi to elaborate on the technique of entering the causal space but he looked at me with hesitation. It was the sort of look one gives a child who asks for knowledge that only an adult can understand. As a matter of compassion, he replied, "Study the embryos. They are meditating on that causal space. That happens while their bodies are prepared. Try to remember your existential status as an embryo."

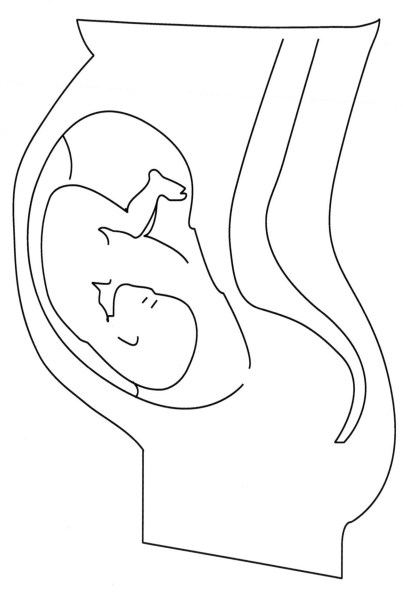

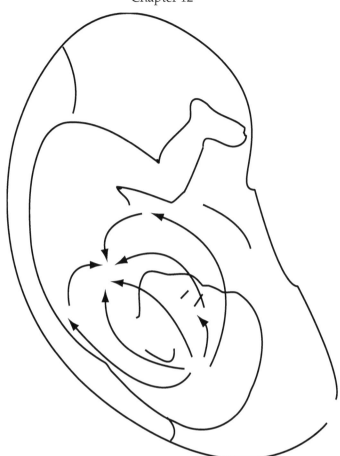

Developing Awareness of the Subtle Body

As long as we transmigrate, we will continue to accept gross bodies. Thus it is necessary to understand how the subtle body operates. In the Bhagavad Gītā, there are verses which establish the eternality of the soul but to verify that eternality is a totally different issue.

One should try to experience the subtle body while the gross one lives. If we do not become established, at least in the subtle body, how will it be possible for us to go beyond that? Whatever trashy impressions are stored in the subtle body will travel on with that body at the time of death. Those impressions will accompany the soul to the next gross form. That next body will begin as a semen particle and then change into an embryo and finally emerge from a womb as a baby form.

Just as we forgot the past life, we will forget these present events, when we take the next body. To prevent this, one should shift to the subtle form and keep the mind focused there more than it is focused on gross reality.

A new gross body will not support all the experience absorbed by the subtle form from past lives. It will however express some of those tendencies in childhood in an unrecognizable form. For instance, if in the previous adult body I ate rich foods, the new infant form may eat dirt. Dirt is not food but the tendency of putting objects into the mouth may surface in that way.

If in the previous adult body I was habituated to leisure and idle time, this might be converted to playful nature, mischievousness and idleness in childhood. An adult form would find leisure by sitting on comfortable couches. The infant form might show this by playing or rolling on the ground. The activity is different but the core tendency is the same.

If I had an important position in society in the previous life, my infant form would express that as distaste for being controlled by parents and as naughty behavior, always going against the will of parents. In this way a great man in a former adult body might express a naughty childhood. It is therefore important to understand how the subtle body functions and to get accustomed to it before the time of death.

The Basic Requirement for Cheating Death

To cheat death and the fear that death involves, one must keep the subtle body in tip-top shape. Cheating death means to be rid of the fear of the final separation between the gross and subtle forms; to be free from the attachments to mundane social relationships which will be disrupted at death. If one is properly anchored in the subtle body, he will not be shocked by the death of the gross one. His point of reference will not change when the gross body dies. Conversely, if one is habituated to focusing through the gross form, one will be forced to execute a shift of priorities at the time of death. The resulting disappointment and frustration will produce emotional shock.

The fear of permanent separation between the gross and subtle bodies arises because we are focused on the gross side to a greater degree. The removal of this fear involves lifting our attention from the gross side, releasing it, and placing it on the subtle side. There is a range of dimensions beyond the earthly plane. If a man can establish relationships with the permanent residents of some of these hereafter places, he would not be lonely at the time of death.

The Causal Body

From our present position on the existential divide, it is difficult to understand the causal form. We cannot perceive its shape, color or location. When we hear of the causal body, we try to perceive it by the intellect and to understand it from the experience of others. The subtle body is difficult to perceive, what to speak of the causal one. As the subtle body is the basis for the gross one, so the causal body is the basis for the subtle one. If I have not experienced the subtle one, I cannot experience the causal one which is more subtle.

In one sense every living being continuously experiences the subtle and gross bodies just as a lamp is continuously experiencing the oil which is drawn through its wick or as a light bulb is continuously aware of the electricity that surges through it. In the conditioned state, due to gross focus, we have little objective understanding of these things.

The causal body accommodates ideation only. It cannot be used to move a gross form directly. It has to work through the agency of the subtle form. To understand the causal body, we must first realize that the causal form cannot move a physical body unless it acts through a subtle one.

The example of air and a sailboat may help us to understand this. If we try to manage a sailboat without erecting sails, we will not do very well. The wind will pass the sail posts without effect. As soon as we install sails, the wind can be utilized. In this example the sails are like the subtle body, the boat itself is like the heavy gross form, and the wind is the causal form which has within it the will power and the idea potential. As long as there is a subtle body between the causal and physical one, we can operate the physical one. In addition, the subtle body must be connected in the proper way. If the subtle body is connected improperly to the nerves and lungs of the gross one, we cannot operate the gross body.

At present we use the spaces, mind and intellect, but we use these in a downward way, focusing downward into the gross form. This focusing downward causes pain and fear at the time of death. If we relax this focus and simply remain detached from the gross level, there will be no separation trauma at the time of death.

The dimension of the causal body is the dimension of the most basic form of intentions and motivations. In the causal world there are no gross material elements and only the invisible material molecules exist there. The causal bodies are spaces within which living entities are housed.

On the level where the subtle body functions, there are no gross forms only flimsy subtle ones. The subtle body develops airy limbs and senses. We can understand this by observing how the wind moves a cloud, or how a gentle breeze moves smoke. A subtle object requires a subtle instrument to handle it.

Having a causal body and not having a subtle one to match it, is like having a desire to do something and not having the means to enact it. There are many living entities who have only causal bodies and none of them can act in the material world unless they acquire subtle forms or unless they influence other entities with subtle bodies to act on their behalf. Only those who are completely free of the need for mundane involvement can remain satisfied with a causal body alone. Otherwise one will, of necessity, develop a subtle form.

The celestial people have no gross bodies because they are satisfied with a causal and subtle form. We have gross forms because we were not satisfied with subtle existence. We were not happy living as subtle energy. We felt the need for the gross earthly bodies.

Those who desire to exist in the mundane world but who effectively resist the need for physical forms, take celestial subtle bodies. They are not satisfied with mere causal forms which only accommodate intentions and motives and which make no efforts to produce even the very subtlest of forms. The celestial people reach a practical level in the production of subtle objects, and their satisfaction and sense of fulfillment is completed there.

Unless a living entity is able to rid the self of the need for the causal, subtle and gross material bodies, he cannot go higher. His needs for mundane existence will prevent him from departing from this place. In that sense everything hinges on purification and elevation of mind.

To escape the gross, one must take shelter in the subtle. This is what the celestials do on a permanent basis. They remain anchored in subtle celestial worlds. To escape the subtle body, one must become sheltered in the causal form. This is what some of the great mystics do. Usually, they do not take rebirth. Sometimes they assume physical forms to demonstrate methods of release.

On the causal plane, one has to be content with mere intentions and motives and that amounts to living in the super-subtle energy. At least this is how it appears, from our perspective.

Understanding the Hereafter

Preparation for passing on from a material body, requires more than familiarity with the subtle form. One must also know something about the lands in the hereafter. The atheists feel there is no hereafter. Some mystics are uncertain about it and feel that everything beyond this gross earthly level is dependent on our minds. Their idea was explained by the sage Vasishtha long, long ago as recorded in the Yoga Vasishtha, a Vedic text which denies God's importance and gives priority to our fanciful mental views. According to such philosophy, ideas such as those of hell are fanciful only, being dependent more or less on the condition of our minds.

If the universal situation of super worlds, worlds and sub-worlds, was dependent on our minds, it could not exist. Anything that is dependent on a limited mind relaxes and loses configuration as soon as that limited mind loses focus. This is quite evident when a person passes on from this gross level and his influence collapses. The influence does not remain the same. In some rare cases, the influence actually increases. Jesus Christ, for instance, increased his influence after he lost the material body. He continued converting people to his ideas. Usually, however, a man's influence rapidly decreases when his body dies.

The dimensions of the earth are not dependent on our puny wills. Some other supreme will is maintaining the earth independently. To say that it depends on my mind or your mind is sheer nonsense, because we are not that important. A prisoner can say what he likes but the prison building is not dependent on him. When he is released, the prison remains. Similarly our mental condition at the time of death does not in any way, affect the dimensions, even though it may affect our response to such places.

We should sort the difference between our response to reality and the reality itself, and not confuse the two. The dimensions are just as real as government prisons. It is not just a matter of what misery or convenience we create in our minds. The misery is created by not observing the laws of nature. As soon as we break these laws we position ourselves for inconvenience.

Hells

This writer had the opportunity to visit a hell recently. This is the hell for men who use prostitutes during their earthly life. At that place, the Hell Police were women with muscular bodies just like women on earth who lift weights and develop muscular physiques. One man arrived there, being dragged by a chain around his neck. He was severely beaten for a time. He was beaten to such an extent that his flesh tore. He was moaning horribly.

Interestingly, he was in a subtle body but the form appeared just as gross to him as his recently departed earthly form. Hence, even though he used a flimsy body, he could not realize it. My subtle body got there by astral projection, but I knew that he was transferred there involuntarily by some other method. As a visitor to that place, I asked a male attendant to show me how the man was brought there. I said, "Please show me exactly how this man's subtle body was brought from the earthly world to this other place. It is hard to believe that he could be brought to this place, especially since his earthly body had just died. Through which dimensional opening was he transferred?"

Then I was shown the door of the act of sexual involvement with prostitutes. In other words, the vice energies formed a subtle doorway through which his soul passed at the time of death.

Then I asked another question because I did not understand how that vice could be converted into a doorway. "How can this man escape? He suffers terribly. I am sure he did not understand the consequences of his activities. Do you think that I could secure his release?"

The attendant said, "He can be helped by any concerned parties such as relatives and friends who still have gross bodies. They can begin atonement for his vices. If they make ample compensations, the energies invested would reach here. Then he would be released. They would have to compensate the society in which he encouraged prostitution. The compensation would have to do with increasing sexual morality in that society, as well as assisting females who are victimized by prostitution and reforming males who are lured into it."

Then I said, "I do not know this man. Neither do I know his relatives. I doubt if they would listen to me. Is there anything else that can affect his release?"

The attendant said, "I am sorry. You were brought here to witness something and to encourage you to explain these developments. Your mission here is not the release of this man. Unless you are related to him it would be very difficult to assist him."

He continued, "Assisting those who come to this hell entails being responsible for their complete reformation. It entails being able to find reformatory parents for them. Can you get this man a birth opportunity? Can you arrange his moral upbringing? We do not think you have the power to arrange these things."

After this my subtle body left that place and returned to this earthly location. I was, all the more, humbled by the experience.

Cross-worlds

Apart from what we experience on this earthly planet, there are parallel worlds or cross-worlds, which are adjacent dimensions in which one may exist either in a subtle or a correspondingly gross form. There are unlimited numbers of these cross-worlds. Some of them are solid like this earthly place and some are shifty like a passing dream state. Human beings regularly enter these cross-worlds but forget the experiences endured. A person, whose mind objectifies and retains subtle activities, can vividly remember the experiences.

Usually one enters a cross-world in a vision, dream and semi-sleepy state. One goes there on the basis of relationships with persons who passed on from the earthly place and who are usually trying to get earthly bodies but were unable to get these for one reason or another. A common reason is their attachment to the departed (dead) form which they lost and which they were so attached to, that they did not adjust to being without it. They still think that they were actually that old material body which passed away. They exist in a cross-world in the same subtle configuration of the old form just like a film negative which retains the image of a picture that was taken long ago. By the power of attachment, one is drawn into their association.

I will mention a few experiences just to show how to determine visitation to a cross-world. During the year of 1994, I was the custodian of a large church complex. One of the buildings was used only once a week for prayer meetings and services. During the rest of each week, that building was vacant. I, as the hired custodian, used to go into the building for cleaning and maintenance. Sometimes on my lunch break he would rest on the floor of the building. Once while resting, my subtle body separated from the gross form and entered a cross-world. Some people who lived in that dimension, arrested me and accused me of moving into their dwelling place.

This was a factual occurrence because the subtle body that the writer used was just as real in that place as the gross one is in this earthly place. The people said, "We live here. You desire to live here. You cannot take our place. Do not rest your body here."

The writer agreed and out of respect, he never rested in that room again. Those cross-world people were formerly members of the church who departed earthly bodies but who were unable to get baby forms. In the dream encounter, after agreeing to their request, my subtle body was released. I felt a very uneasy, haunted feeling although I bore no resentment.

Later on, another person, a woman who was hired as a cleaner, complained that she did not like to go into the building alone. She felt that it was spooked and haunted. She said, "Sometimes doors slam even though all windows are closed and forceful air cannot enter. Sometimes I hear noises. Sometimes it seems that someone walks through the building even though I see no one."

Understanding that the woman sensed the cross-world people and not wanting to reinforce her fears, I denied everything. I replied, "There is no one in the building. You are sensitive to atmospheric pressure. Take no worry of it."

The woman, unknown to herself, had some psychic sense and actually heard those things on the psychic level but she confused psychic hearing with physical hearing. It is easy to mistake a purely psychic experience for a physical one. The subtle body which experiences the psychic world, is interspaced into the gross body whenever the gross body is awake. Experiences detected by the subtle form are regularly mistaken for gross reality.

Soon after this, a male elderly member of the church, shot his body and passed on from it. He was terribly depressed over his aged form. Since he felt that his body was himself, he shot the body to get out of the depressed condition, without understanding that the depression would continue in the subtle form even after the gross one was destroyed.

Before one commits suicide, one should know that a human being has several layers of identity. There is the perishable human or creature form that we see. There is a supernatural psychology, namely the eternal soul, the mind, emotions, and subtle life impulses. These subtle, psychological parts do not perish but go with each of us beyond death. A human being is actually a combination of the personality, psychological energy and perishable body.

Some people feel that a human being is just a body and the frail mind. They do not perceive the core personality as a separate feature. They feel that the body and mind will not survive death and that mental confusion and misery will be terminated at death. Some propose that the body and the frail, subtle constituents vanish while only the soul survives. These are mistaken notions. The gross body definitely dies but the soul and subtle constituents survive. In suicide, the mind and emotions survive. Suicide is not a solution to emotional or mental problems.

In any case, this male member who shot his body, passed on and then came back to the church and began living in a particular room where a prayer meeting was held each Sunday. He used to stay there in an astral form that looked exactly like his old physical body.

Once by the force of his former membership in the church, he acquired a power to pull my subtle body into the cross-world he inhabited. He warned the writer. He said, "This is our room. We built it. We spent our money on it. This is our religion. Do not rest your body in this room again." The writer agreed and the man released my subtle body.

In yet another experience, the writer found himself in a cross-world speaking to an elderly woman whom he knew when his body was in its boyhood. This particular lady passed on from this earthly place and after some 30 years she still had not acquired a gross human form, but she was living in a parallel world in a house which was a replica of the one she used on earth. Interestingly, the place had the same streets, the same kind of muddy clay, and the same kind of market places. When I arrived, the lady acted as if I would stay there forever. She began talking as if she had never passed on and as if I were a permanent resident of that place, even though it was a parallel astral land and not the original earth she lived on. And besides, she passed on 30 years ago. When I tried to leave she held my subtle body there, but I knew that she could not hold it forever. I kept relating to her and as soon as she relaxed, I left the place.

There are other similar experiences and not all of them are of a lowly kind, involving lowly entities. After the departure of a great spiritual master, one may meet such a great soul in higher dimensions, cross-worlds which exist all in themselves and which are just as real, in fact more real, than this earthly place. After the departure of the great Vaishnava spiritual leader, *Śrīla A.C. Bhaktivedānta Swāmī Prabhupada*, the writer had many meetings with him in various parallel dimensions but a particular experience stands out. In this one, the great authority had just departed from his physical body and was passing through the subtle atmosphere on the way to a higher place. Some angelic beings, were melodiously praising him. They were singing a song I had not heard before, namely:

- *jai prabhu prabhu gorachan*
- *prabhu kanandana gorachan*

They kept repeating this song to the accompaniment of sweet celestial music never heard on earth. This is a song in the Sanskrit language and even though at the time, I was not very familiar with Sanskrit, he remembered the words clearly and jotted them down as soon as he returned to earthly consciousness. Later on I considered the meaning.

jai prabhu:	All glories unto you, O great spiritual master!
prabhu gorachan:	O lordly master, who glorified the sacred sandalwood pulp and the five sacred products produced from the body of cows.
prabhu kanandana gorachan:	O master of the living entities. O you, who are so dear to Vaishnava devotees of the Lord and who is known for usage of the five sacred products produced from the body of cows!

In the experience, I found myself in a celestial form in which the *amṛta* nectar of the celestials was experienced in a great intensity of spiritual happiness. The vision of that body was super-keen. All the mystic powers were available for usage through it. It floated through the air and was not impeded.

By having such experiences before the time of death, all of one's fears about death are removed and one understands clearly that there is no death of soul or of the mind which is the reservoir of tendencies. One will continue to exist and will have relationships in realistic environments after leaving the gross body. There is absolutely no shortage of these parallel worlds.

Money and Spiritual Practice

Each ascetic should carefully check the results of practice. One should not leave it up to others to track advancement. One should not become complacent, confident or lazy, nor should one feel that one will progress merely because the religion or discipline is supposed to yield results.

It is also a mistake to feel that easy material living, easy access to money, easy influence over others, are signs of spiritual success.

Usually one gains access to money on the basis of piety from past lives and on the basis of a monetary sense of direction and not on the basis of a particular religion. For instance, a person with sufficient piety and organizational skills may have easy access to money regardless of which family or society his body is derived from. Regardless of whether he is indoctrinated in the Christian, Hindu or Muslim religion, he will have access to money. This means that it is based directly on piety and financial aptitude.

Chapter 13

In meditation, one discovers a personal way of settling the mind. And even though settling the mind is not meditation, it is a beginning for those who desire to meditate. Settling the mind is a preparatory activity for meditation. Each person should find a practical method so that one can free the self daily from the rigors of mental association.

Hunches

Reincarnation is verified by memory of former existences, but even if there is no recall, memory is still involved in meditation. Memory is a reference point from which to flee for meditation. In meditation, the impressions stored as memory should not be allowed to harass the meditator. These mental impressions and their instincts are in the psyche, but they should lie still as if they are afraid to disturb the meditator. If they are activated during meditation, the meditation is disrupted. The self either pursues the subject of memory or silences it by an effective discipline. An understanding of reincarnation is necessary for successful meditation. Before we reach a state of meditation, we have to pass through several layers of memory. If we are not aware of reincarnation, the memories will cause us to make false conclusions, which obstruct the meditation.

Hunches or ideas of past lives can be recorded. Then the seeker may double check to ascertain if his interpretations were correct. He can read historic studies about people and places and gauge his understanding to see if the hunches are correct.

He can visit places which he thought were known to him in a past life. He can gauge his preconceptions of these. Hunches are subconscious hints but they may not be accurate. They should be verified either with historic data or with visitations. One should neither trust the subconscious stockpile of memories nor be neglectful of it. But one should be up and about, verifying its presentations within the conscious mind.

Ancestral Influence

Each human being has flashes of past life relationships with others. Even with strangers, one may get the feeling of having known the person before. Even with a person whose body is of the same age, one may get the feeling of having been related to the person as an elder or junior. I once knew a lady. Even though her body was the same age as mine, she related to me as if I were her son or nephew. Even though she was not my senior in knowledge, she always looked over me with a protective gaze. Her subtle body tried to assert a relationship from a past life when she was a social senior. Just as today a father can beget the body for a person who is his superior in capacity, so she tried to dominate the relationship as if she were my protector.

In another example, a woman whose body was 15 years my senior, treated me as if I was her boyfriend. From the bodily level, it was a mismatch. Still, she tried and tried and went through the romantic motions emotionally. Her subtle body recognized mine as a previous lover. It impulsively tried to manifest that relationship.

In yet another example, a woman who was some 20 years my senior, experienced feelings of affection for me, just as if I were her husband. Being embarrassed and knowing that she did not dare to compromise social rules, she presented me with her daughter, a girl who felt little attraction to me. The girl fiercely resisted her mother's idea. The mother's subtle body tried to use the daughter's physical form as its agent for completing a romantic idea from a past life.

When there are sexual connotations, the subtle body becomes very assertive. It may even risk social disgrace. It may exert itself and produce a loss of reputation. This occurs because of a lusty impulsion to complete unfulfilled relationships from past lives.

The current high rate of divorce is the assertion of the subtle bodies trying to fulfill more than one conjugal fantasy in a lifetime. Morality usually permits each person only one marriage partner, but the subtle bodies try to break that restriction.

Pressure from Departed Souls

The world of the living is not separated from the world of the dead, but those who are living feel that they took possession of the rights of the dead. In most cases, however, they have only taken possession of the responsibilities which were to be completed by the dead. In the first place, those who are dead, live on in the psychic world. This psychic world, which is called the hereafter, is experienced by us as the mental-emotional world of feelings, conceptions, and ideas.

Since we are simultaneously situated in the mento-emotional and the physical world, we have an advantage over the dearly departed. They do not have direct physical contact. This advantage of ours, however, is converted into a disadvantage since our focus into this world decreases our perception of the psychic world. The departed souls, or so-called dead people, have a greater psychic capacity. They are in a position to influence us through emotions and thoughts.

Once I had a friend who had this idea that he wanted to be a great landlord. His idea was to own a city block of buildings. He felt he would own such buildings, rent them, and become wealthy thereby. Unfortunately, some of this mental energy leaked into my nature. Even though it was not my ambition, still in his association I felt that I too should become a great landlord. Years after when I remembered the association, I realized that it was not my friend who influenced me, but it was his ancestors. They transmitted the desire to me, in the hope that I would become compatible to their destiny, and that my friend and I would beget bodies for them in two wealthy families.

To their view, both my friend and I were potential fathers. They wanted us to provide opportunities for their return to this world in families with political and financial power.

When this body was about 13 years old, I had a friend who was born in a wealthy family. I was born in a poor family of black-colored bodies. He was in a wealthy family of East Indian descent. He had much excess money. He bet on horses. I had no excess money. He used to share money with me for betting on horses. He would say, "Study the chart. Pick your horse and bet. If you win, we keep the money. We may amass a fortune. When we get older, we will join together and run a large business."

His family ran a fabric store. In that case, it was not my friend. It was his ancestors who tried to prepare us as future fathers. At the time I did not realize it. As providence would have it, the association was broken. I had to leave the country.

Many of us are fooled by this ancestral influence. We think that we act independently, while in fact we function as mere puppets of the desires of others. For their sake, we may commit violence and act irresponsibly.

Quality of Mental Energy

Yoga practice is said to have eight stages, namely:

yama:	*restraints from immoral behavior*
niyama:	*observances of moral behavior*
āsana:	*postures*
prāṇāyāma:	*breath enrichment*
pratyāhara:	*sensual energy retraction*
dhāraṇā:	*linkage of attention to a higher person or energy*
dhyāna:	*effortless linkage of attention to a higher person or energy.*
samādhi:	*continuous effortless linkage of attention to a higher person or energy.*

The stage of *āsanas* means mastering the physical body to make it as healthy and as energy-efficient as possible. Since the soul's energy is involved in operating the body, efficient use of the energy means that the soul would provide less power for bodily maintenance. It will in turn have more energy to invest in spiritual realization.

After perfecting *āsanas*, one should practice breath enrichment. Normally a human being regards food as nutrition and air as a life energy. Both air and food are nutritional, however. Both are supportive of life energy. The practice of *prāṇāyāma* causes more efficient energy usage of the subtle body.

A healthy body uses less energy than a diseased one, and a healthy astral or subtle body uses less energy than a lazy, polluted one. All this concerns conservation of soul energy. The more energy we conserve, the more we can invest in spiritual realization.

After perfecting *āsanas* postures and *prāṇāyāma* breath nutrition methods, an ascetic develops mind control. His focus increases. Still, one cannot adjust the quality of the energy in the mind merely by concentration. Changing the quality of the energy in the mind is a separate accomplishment. Concentration means focusing the energy in the mind, not changing it. Focused energy is better than the unfocused type, but that has little to do with the quality of the energy. Certain types of intense focus do slightly change the quality of the energy but they do not change it fundamentally. For such change, one needs to perfect the *prāṇāyāma* breath techniques which change gases in the physical body and the subtle gases or *prāṇa* in the subtle form.

Unless an ascetic concentrates with a pure grade of energy, he cannot get total control of thoughts nor can he control his responses to incoming thoughts. By any amount of concentration, one will gain some control, but a little control is not mastership; it is haphazard and unreliable. It causes us to have confidence at one moment and to lose that confidence in the next instant when we give in to random ideas.

Regardless of whether we are dealing with self-produced thoughts or with foreign ideas which entered the mind, the crucial issue is the quality of the mental energy we possess. A low quality of mental energy means greater lack of control. With a low quality of energy we can neither resist chaotic thoughts, nor properly analyze the urges which produce haphazard thinking. As such, without thought control, we will continue to act impulsively.

The life energy in the body automatically detects thoughts, just as a radio utilizes radio waves. Usually, we can neither detect how the life energy receives these thoughts nor how it processes them quickly to produce urges which force us to act. However if one improves the quality of the life energy, one develops the sensitivity to detect the sources of the thoughts and to formulate logical and sensible responses to these.

Once a friend became attracted to another friend's wife. He became obsessed with the beauty and educational capacity of the woman. Later, he began to think of how he could secretly associate with the lady. He did not speak to me about it. By the closeness of our friendship, I detected his thinking.

Later on that day, he began to think that I should invite the lady to a meeting when her husband was absent. I detected this thought. Even though he never said a word to me, I knew that it developed in his mind. He never asked me since he instinctively knew that I would object to the plan. It is not that I am above such thoughts, but I have the ability to analyze and discard them if I see that ultimately they are not in my interest or that even if they are in my interest, they are not worth the social disruption they might cause.

In that situation, the life energy of my friend not only influenced him but also acted to influence me. Thus the life energy is powerful and effective in terms of motivating and urging someone to permit reckless, irresponsible acts.

Incidentally, the woman also was at fault. On one occasion when I saw her in the presence of this friend, she deliberately but carefully displayed their romantic attraction to me.

Considering this, we can see that the soul has to be very careful in the urges it sponsors and in what activities it allows its gross or subtle body to complete. It should realize the limitations. There are some activities which are not in our interest and which we helplessly perform anyway, all to our detriment. Even if we achieve only a fraction more restraint over the impulsive nature, the effort for self-control is well worth it.

Thought Tracking

Thought tracking is a necessary activity for those who want mind control. Incoming thoughts usually enter the mind without detection. The mind is open to these thoughts. Even while sleeping, these thoughts enter the mind and affect rest or dreaming. Have you ever been dreaming and then found that your dream was abruptly changed to another unrelated scene? Then later, after rising, you meet someone who said something that is the exact replica of a conversation from the non-related dream.

Here is an example. Once I worked as a kitchen hand. I used to carry supplies into a large kitchen. One day I fell asleep during my work time in a back room. While resting, my dream was abruptly switched to a scene where the head cook asked me to carry some items. Then all of a sudden, I awoke and heard someone in another part of the building. To avoid being caught asleep, I quickly got up and returned to work. As I went, the head cook called. He instructed me to carry some items. These things were the same items my subtle body carried in the dream.

In that case, the cook's thought penetrated my dream. His forceful idea affected me to such an extent that my subtle body executed the instruction on the psychic plane. Then I repeated the action physically.

In some dreams, however, when there is a switch from one dream to another, the new dream becomes distorted or mixed with the first and the dreamer perceives that combination in a confused way.

Here is an example.

A student of mine kept a dream journal. In one entry she related a dream where she found herself at a shopping mall. She stood at a check-out counter and told a person how she enjoyed the idea of taking her children shopping even though usually she soon became disgusted with their behavior. While she explained this, the children drifted out of sight.

At the end of the conversation, someone whom she recognized approached her. This was a friend from a spiritual community where she lived previously. The friend took her around a corner to a gathering of other community members. The majority were dressed in East Indian clothing. One woman carried a tray of food. Then suddenly in the dream, the dreaming lady remembered the children. Feeling they were lost in the mall, she became anxious to locate them.

This dream recall was of two dreams blended into one. The first occurred at the mall with her children and the other one was in another subtle dimension with members of a spiritual community. While dreaming, the lady was not aware of her departure from the mall. She thought she was near the mall the entire time.

It was not until she analyzed the dream some weeks later that she objectively separated it into two separate encounters.

In another dream of hers, the confusion was greater:

She had keys to a house and entered it, leaving the door unlocked behind her. No one was inside. She passed through and turned off light switches, fans and electrical appliances. One lamp issued smoke and she called for water.

Even though she did not see medication, she sensed that pills were in the room. Someone called to ask her for a prescription form from a stack of papers.

A stumpy, dark-skinned man entered and warned that she should not have come. He said that thieves would steal everything after she left. As she stood there, she saw men coming in and going out, taking items from the house.

When she analyzed this entry later on, she sorted it into more than one dream. The first part occurred at a place of employment. She had keys to a large building where she was employed once per week to secure the premises and turn off all electrical equipment. She returned to that job location in the subtle world.

The second dream began with her sensing of pills in a room. She was at a doctor's office or medical clinic. When the dark-bodied person arrived, she was in a third dream, at a location where the moving or theft occurred.

As the dreamer, however, she felt that this occurred at the first building where she turned off the electricity. She recorded it in her journal as a single dream at a single location. During later analysis, she sorted the confusion.

Until recall is clear, there is bound to be confusion. Other people in the dreams may be misidentified or not recognized at all. The subtle world is hard to analyze; flash events occur quickly. One dream may conclude or a person may instantly move into a new encounter by a slight impulse or distraction. The transitions may go unnoticed by the dreamer.

The subtle body is more impulsive and difficult to control than the physical one. A high degree of mystic perceptiveness and self-control would develop by recording dreams. This would increase the ability to sort chaotic and seemingly meaningless encounters.

Incoming thoughts enter the mind undetected. The sensual energy reacts to these automatically, and a conclusion is created by the intellect. The intellect then shows the soul some ideas. The soul usually permits the intellect to signal the body to act on the opinions.

The Life Force and Problems

Problems remain in the mind until they are settled satisfactorily. A man cannot meditate if he has problems. He cannot get rid of problems without simplification of desires and a scaling down of arrogance. Any problem in the mind may be subjected to energization by the life energy in the subtle body. Once the life energy becomes linked to a problem, we become engrossed in thought of how to outwit unfavorable circumstances. Even so-called religious men are involved in this outwitting business. After becoming fatigued, they say, "I am tired of the hassles. I want to go away from it all." Actually, they are not tired, nor do they want to go away. They are in love with the perplexing energies.

When a man is really tired, he develops a need for simplification of desires by scaling down plans from an elephant-size operation to an ant-size one.

There is a meditation technique where one shuts down the waking impulse in the brain. This impulse is triggered from the pons area of the brain as shown below.

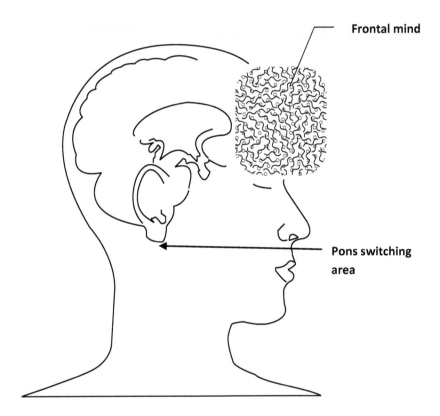

Frontal mind

Pons switching area

Normally we feel that the waking impulse might be in the center or frontal lobe of the brain. This is because we operate most of the senses from a centralized position in the brain. However, the energy that electrifies the brain comes from the spinal column. This energy passes through a switch in the pons area. By training oneself to regulate this switch, one can gain more control over the rest-work, awake-sleep cycles of the body.

Since we are usually oriented to the frontal lobe of the brain, we are not in the habit of looking into the back area of it. The frontal lobe has the optic circuitry and the planning faculty. Most of our energy goes to the frontal lobe, even though it is not in our interest to maintain too much of an energy flow in that area. In the effort for simplification, we should move our attention to the back of the brain. If you ever get some time, try to shift your awareness from within the brain, so that you look out the back of the head.

The following series of diagrams may assist you. First try to sense the subtle head within the gross one. Realize the subtle head within the space of the physical one.

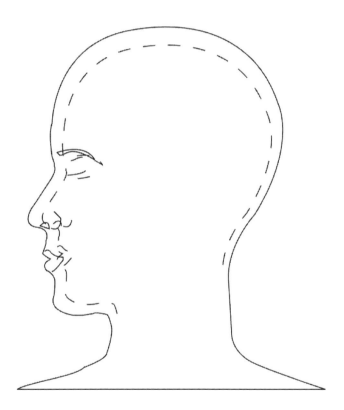

Turn the subtle head sideways over the shoulder

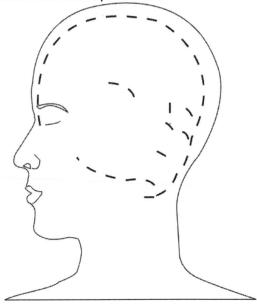

Completely turn the subtle head profile to look straight back through the gross head!

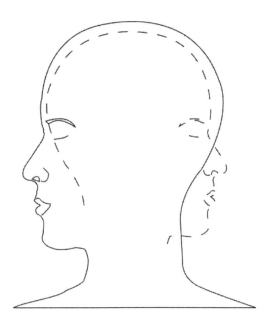

The Radio of the Mind

Long before the advent of radio, human beings broadcasted ideas through the mind. Most of us do this unconsciously, not realizing the transmission. Long before movies and television, we used the movie screen of the mind. A modern invention called Virtual Reality projects images in such a way that an audience may interact with it, just as if it were real. A man who has no girlfriend may attend a party and dance with a projected image of an attractive woman.

These aspects were being played out in the mind long before this technology was developed. In addition, the animals also have that mental power. They also imagine within the mind. Do you feel that a mouse does not dream? Do you feel that a mouse does not think or is not influenced by thoughts from other thinkers in its own and other species?

If the life energy in the psyche is clean and of a high quality, the mind sorts high energy and low energy thoughts. If it picks up low energy thoughts, it presents these with clarity for analysis by the intellect. If, however, the life energy is of low quality, the mind detects only lower energy thoughts. And whatever it takes in from low-energy sources is presented in a distorted way through which the intellect analyzes incorrectly.

The mind also picks up images while the body sleeps and even while the soul is absent from the body during sleep. The soul may stay interposed in a sleeping body or it may leave that body temporarily. For such temporary absences from the body, the soul uses the astral form.

When the astral form leaves the body, most of the mind energy separates from the body. A small portion remains with the physical form and absorbs psychic information. If, for instance, your body is sleeping in the United States and your astral form interacts somewhere in China, you might be abruptly drawn back into the physical form if someone near the sleeping body calls your name. The portion of the mind that remained with the sleeping body, will instantly transmit a recall energy. Then your life energy will direct the astral form back into the physical body. This happens instantly since the astral form can travel at the speed of light. It will appear magical since the return to the United States occurred in an instant.

If you were not aware of the separation of your astral form while you were in China, you might think that you were dreaming of being in China and that you heard someone calling and awoke suddenly.

Just as a thought would reach a man who is temporarily separated from his body, so a thought reaches him also when he is consciously awake on the physical side. This is all done by the telepathic powers of the mind. Since we are focused on the material side, subtle vibrations do not register clearly. We fail to realize how sensitive the mind really is. By studying modern inventions like the telephone and radio, we can get some hints.

In the system of the telephone we can learn much about the operation of the mind. If, for instance, a man is away from home, a family member might try to reach him mentally. This is done by thinking of him and mostly by thinking to present an idea, suggestion or question to him. When that idea is formulated, it is automatically transmitted to him. If, for instance, a telephone receiver is switched on, it will transmit anything a man says before it, even if the man is unaware that his speech was broadcast. Similarly, except when the body is in a coma, the mind, which is always switched on, transmits thoughts through the atmosphere.

We are always absorbing the thoughts of others. We absorb images and concepts. Usually we identify these as our own views or as random concoctions of the mind.

Life Force

The life force produces and enforces exploitive demands. The soul senses the demands and randomly permits the life force to use the mind, intellect and senses, to execute the required action. It is the life energy or motivation instinct that does all this. Its needs are verbalized in the mind as conceptions and language symbols, or externally as the primitive grunts and squeaks of the animals.

The spirit-self does not have the need for exploitation. It is not a shifty energy. It is affected because it is linked to the life energy. That link cannot be broken by wishful thinking. One has to take a set course of austerities under the direction of a liberated entity.

Dream Recall

Keep a journal by your bedside. Jot down thoughts, ideas, and dreams that you recall upon awakening. Review the journal from time to time to see what consistent or inconsistent dreams or ideas you have while the body rests or sleeps. This simple procedure increases awareness in dreams. Increased awareness of the dream world is a step in the direction of being more aware of psychic body. After all, if you leave the gross form permanently, an increased awareness of the psychic world, will be an asset for you.

By dream recall one can judge spiritual progress. Whatever discipline one follows, should be tested on the mystic plane. If, for instance, I try to resist sex desire and I achieve quite a degree of control in the physical world, I may find that in dreams I have little or no resistance. In the physical world, I may carefully avoid breaking moral rules but that does not mean that I am doing so in the psychic world. And if I am not, then I can realize that my disciplines have not penetrated my nature thoroughly. They were acted out only on the surface of my self. Knowing this, I can strive harder or acquire more effective methods.

Bad Ventilation / Bad Dreams

Years ago I noticed that when my body rested in a room with poor ventilation, without a steady flow of fresh air, I had spooky dreams. I decided to study this to be sure that my conclusions were correct.

In this study, I drew the following conclusions:

- *A low life energy supply causes a low energization of the subtle body.*
- *Insufficient fresh air causes inefficient operation of the subtle form.*

I regularly observe that when the physical body rested in a poorly-ventilated room, I have bad dreams. This means that my subtle body became irresistibly drawn to bad association. In addition, if there was much fresh air, I rarely had unpleasant dreams.

If the physical body is sick and is unable to absorb air through the lungs efficiently, I have an increase in discomforting dreams. This is due to the rapid exhaustion of the subtle form. People who are addicted to degrading association, unconsciously pollute their gross and subtle bodies by eating foods which cause the bodies to function in dullness and depression. This is why people use alcohol and depressants. This is why people overeat, even good food, or take good foods and cook them in a de-energizing way.

Psychic Gyrating Centers

The psychic gyrating centers, called the chakras in Sanskrit, have importance because they tell us of the condition of the subtle body. Yogis check the condition of the chakras and gauge spiritual progression by the high or low energization of these gyrating centers. If one attained purity, the chakras would be super-charged.

Psychic Gyrating Centers

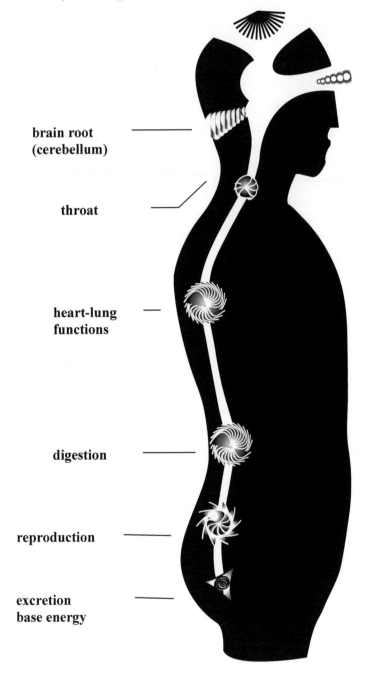

brain root
(cerebellum)

throat

heart-lung
functions

digestion

reproduction

excretion
base energy

One idea is the opening of the chakras. Another is their energization. Yet another idea is the removal of impurity. Each approach has value, depending on the stage of practice.

The idea of opening the chakras, is based on the view that every person has chakras which are closed, semi-closed, or open. Some yogis advise visualization to open the chakras. However most beginners never visually see the chakras or even feel the energy centers. Still, the chakras are a reality since many reliable yogis and even Lord Krishna in teachings to Uddhava, described them.

The idea of energization of the chakras is a view of some yoga teachers who feel that if we could increase the *prāṇa* or subtle energy reaching to a chakra, it would operate on a higher level. This idea is similar to the idea of increasing the current going to a dim light bulb. If the current is increased the filament will brighten. Some yogis tell their students, "Your chakras have a low charge. You need to energize the subtle body. Take up these disciplines. Change your way of life. Associate with me at this ashram and the desired energization will occur."

Following this advice, some students find that their minds are not enlightened. Some get or feel a charge for a day or two and then find that they lapse to the old drag-along consciousness. Many Western youths see chakras visually when they take stimulants or hallucinogenic drugs. Some of these try yoga, get no instant result, and return to the sure way of drug-induced altered consciousness to see the many lights and energy gyrations of the numerous chakras which are in every life form in the creation. Having discovered for themselves that yoga did not give instant results, they return to a seemingly quicker method by drug-induced adjustment of their psychic perception.

The idea of cleaning the chakras of impurity has to do with the belief that bad diet and immoral habits have caused the chakras to become impure. Thus if we adopt a moral way of life and change diet, certain energy centers improve. These adjustments, however, must be coupled with yoga techniques and *prāṇāyāma* breath regulation practices for improvement of the chakras.

Yogis, sometimes pass through the third eye chakra to enter various higher dimensions, especially into the pure spiritual energy and the world of that domain. A reverse process pulls the spiritual energy into the psyche through the brow chakra. Here is a diagram:

In this practice, instead of leaving one's mind field, one pulls spiritual energy into it and cleanses it from within.

I may cry out to a teacher for a technique but when I get it, I may not use it or I may use it for some time, and then put it aside. Without techniques I cannot make advancement.

Yogis usually share realization. When a lesser yogi meets a greater one, the lesser yogi opens himself to new information. The trick is to get techniques. In some aspects of spiritual life, one listens carefully for newer, better-sounding promises of salvation, but in yoga, one listens for techniques. No matter what a teacher tells us, if he does not give methods for direct experience, we do not progress.

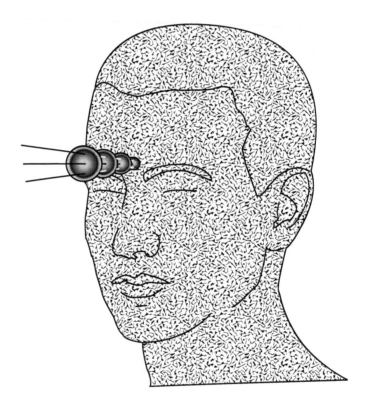

The Crown Chakra

For most people, the crown chakra is inactive. This is due to sharp material focus and heavy reliance on the material world. Because we are determined to conquer the gross world, the crown chakra is shut down. It will take deliberate endeavor to open that region of the mind. We can begin the process by developing the brow chakra and then gradually one may focus on the higher areas of the brain, beginning with the top inner forehead.

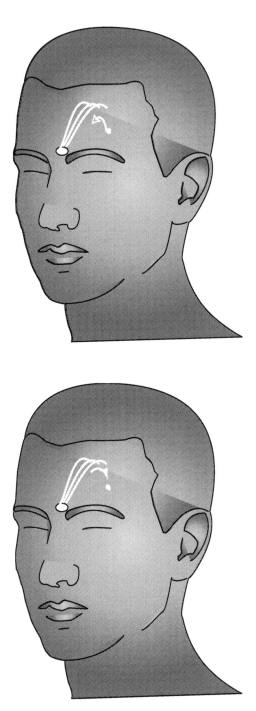

Meditate on inner forehead. Generate energy there.

Some teachers stress the vision of the outer starlight. This is a light seen when all the energies in the subtle body are perfectly balanced. This is seen at the brow chakra. For most of us, the subtle energies are rarely balanced. When they do attain quiescence, it occurs momentarily and spontaneously. Yogis, however, have found ways of deliberately balancing the psychic energies.

First, the energies must be purified. That is the preliminary stage. In *prāṇāyāma* practice, a yogi might spend years cleaning the subtle body of its acquired contamination. Then after some time, he develops a pure focus through which he sees the outer starlight. Even so, any of us, without yoga practice, might accidentally and momentarily see the starlight.

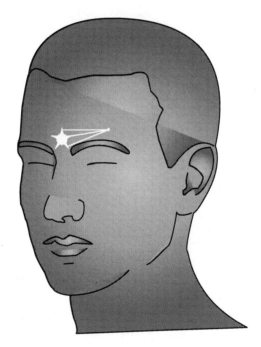

In this diagram the focal consciousness of the soul is located at the psychic center of the mind. The star is positioned slightly beyond the facial plane in the lower forehead region.

Sometimes the star is viewed at a higher position, even near the top of forehead. For most of us the appearance of this star would be accidental and momentary. As such we may not observe it, or even observe the spiritual peace it brings with it. This may occur in the daylight, when our physical eyes are open. Thus, we may hardly perceive it or be aware of it.

The spiritual security some accomplished yogis feel when deliberately viewing this star, is so compelling that many of the yogis consider the vision of this star to be the ultimate experience. Many others who have merely heard of it, spend years trying to reach it, stabilize their vision of it, and remain forever gazing at it. Some say that the star is inside the subtle body. Some say that it is on the outside. It depends on the purity of the yogi who gazes at it. Some say that they have gone through the star into the pure spiritual energy. And some claim they passed through it into the spiritual world.

This writer can say something from personal experience. The star comes and goes of its own accord. Actually, this coming and going is not a movement. The star is stationary. When a ship moves away from a pier, an observer may feel as if the landscape drifted while in fact it was the ship which moved. As in the case of our planetary perspective, we may feel that the sun orbits the earth, while in fact the earth makes the orbit. The mystic star remains where it is. Periodically, we come within its purview.

In some cases in broad daylight, the star appears but it may not be seen or felt. I use the word "appears", because from our limited perspective, that is how we would experience it. When the star appears in darkened mental space, it is readily seen. It appears at first as a tiny speck in the distance. It may be surrounded by pitch blackness, grayness, deep blueness, light blueness, sunshine, or haze.

From time to time, the psychic energies become balanced of their own accord, just as sometimes, the weather becomes favorable. We have no control over it. The yogis put themselves into a state of balance. As soon as they achieve that and for as long as they can maintain that, the star is seen. Yogis who can keep the energies in the central spinal column of the subtle body balanced, can do this.

Śrī Paramhansa Yogānanda, a kriyā yoga master of repute, an influential personality, set many people on the quest of this starlight. In a sense he misled them. People who try to follow him cannot see this star unless they develop mastery of āsana postures and prāṇāyāma breath enrichment, an achievement which Paramhansa Yogānanda gained in his youth.

People like Paramhansa Yogānanda are exceptionally gifted individuals with a long history of yoga austerities in their past and present lives. Unless one has a similar background of austerities, the appearance of this star is not guaranteed. Previously the yogis performed austerities in caves in pitch darkness. In such darkness without any visual distraction, they saw the star, attained a steady gaze on it, and kept themselves in that spiritual communion for hours, days, months, or years, according to their period of isolation.

A man with worries, a man who has a business concerns, and who is not thoroughly free from thinking of the business, cannot see the star. A materialistic man cannot see the star. A confused, crazy fellow cannot see the star. Even yogis of little accomplishment can only see it momentarily and accidentally. It is that difficult to get the psychic energies in balance.

If I go to a lonesome place where there is no modernization, even then I may not be able to see the star if my destiny was not resolved sufficiently. I used to meditate for 30 or 60 minute periods years ago. At the time I did not have much of a practice of *prāṇāyāma*. My subtle body was not as purified as it is now. My celibate practice did not begin in earnest. Still I was meditating for long periods, even though my body was not sitting at ease in the lotus posture. At first I used to put my body in a dark closet. This is how I kept the optic nerves calm. In the beginning of the meditation practice, one cannot achieve much if the optic nerves are being activated by light. I used to go into a dark closet. If no such closet was available and if there was daylight, or if there was an electric light that I could not turn off, I used a dark, cotton cloth to cover my brain and eyes.

One day in the astral world, I met a yogi. Years later I understood that this yogi was *Śrīla Yogeswarananda*. He said, "As long as you have social associations and the resulting problems, you cannot hold the star. Continue the disciplines but do not expect to view it often. It is there in the brow chakra but you will not see it. Have confidence in it. Later on, if your providence is resolved sufficiently by teaching and by completion of austerities, you will see it. You can focus on the brow chakra but do not waste your time and energy thinking that you will see it. If it appears, be satisfied but do not hanker. Solve out your destiny. Face the circumstances that are set before you. Live in a way that reduces the consequential reactions."

These were important instructions, which marked a turning point for me.

Unless the optic nerves are calmed in darkness and through a simplified life, it is not possible to see the star. This simplified life is the non-complicated, honest way of generating an income. If the brain is being taxed to make a dollar, one will not see the star. The psychic energies will never be balanced by continued plotting and the resultant complexities.

Years ago when I had time to meditate and when my life was not complicated by family responsibilities, I used to see the star for a short time.

The star itself would enlarge and open up and I would see out into the spiritual atmosphere.

Initial star-speck

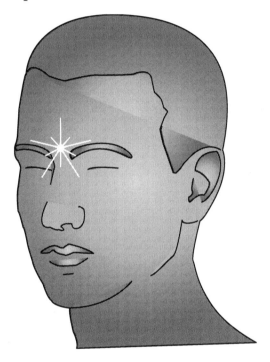

Star-speck enlarges and opens

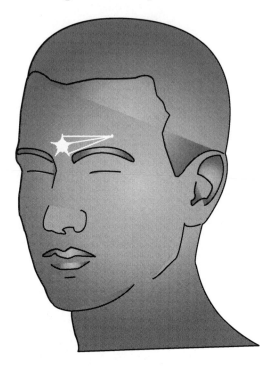

As soon as I developed reproductive interests, my mystic ability decreased proportionately. At a certain point when romantic affairs became intense, it almost ceased entirely. When children came, everything came to a grinding halt. Since I was instructed firmly by Śrīla Yogeshwarananda, I continued the practice. I did not lose faith even though I did not experience results. I knew that whatever disciplines I maintained, would stay with me and that after family duties decreased, I would be free to complete the practice.

As I said earlier, the star used to open. At the time, the brow chakra would open daily, especially around the noon hour and even in daylight. However, perception through it in the daylight is not as clear as in darkness. If the chakra opens, one sees into far away places or in other dimensions of this world, but when the star opens one sees into the spiritual atmosphere. That is the difference. This is why the kriyā yogis are so eager to see the star. The star is a gateway through which we pass to the spiritual places, either to the undifferentiated spiritual atmosphere of bliss consciousness or to varied spiritual lands in the spiritual universe.

The following diagrams may help readers to differentiate between the locations of the brow chakra and the appearance of the star.

The brow chakra is situated inside of the mind space just behind the center of the eyebrows. It may be shaped like a donut, a spiral or a spiked disc. It may appear visually as a ring of bright yellow or goldish light.

Brow Chakra visibility

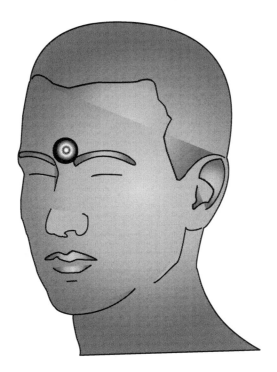

The star appears outside of the gross body and mind space. It appears outside the skull, slightly above the brow center.

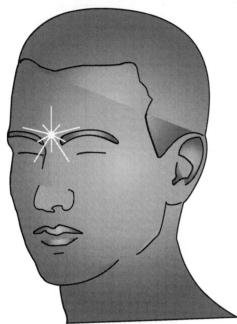

Once in 1973 I had some students. I was meditating for long periods each day. I opened a small ashram. One of the students asked me why it was that she could not realize the brow chakra. What a question it was! Here, I was teaching yoga and meditation, but I was stalled by the question. Other students looked up when she asked the question. And I just stood there. Up to this day I have not answered.

If having family responsibilities caused a termination in the vision of the star, then what would happen if I opened a business and became preoccupied with employees and money? I could just imagine how washed out my spiritual life would be. It would be a case of "be in this world and be condemned in it."

Recently *Śrīla Yogeswarananda* told me that even though I am still trapped in the householder responsibilities, I should still remember that the star is there. He said:

"Do not worry about householder responsibilities. It is temporary. As soon as it is over, intensify the practice. In the meantime, maintain the disciplines. Always know that the starlight is soothing to you. It is shining on you. It is shining down from outside of the causal form.

"Even though it is perceived from the subtle body, it is actually external to the causal form. At present you are restricted to an isolated causal heart cove, closed off as it were, in a dense chamber. But when that chamber opens, the opening of it takes the shape of that star."

He then told me that as the higher tube emerges from the causal body, the star is formed on the very tip of it. If the gross body is reclined, the star would be positioned as shown in this diagram.

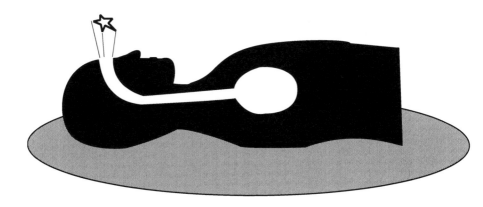

One should meditate, knowing that the star is at the brow chakra. One should not be disheartened because one does not perceive it. One should meditate routinely. Calm the optic nerves. Unless the optic energies are calmed, one will never experience the required balance which harmonizes the clashing energies, which deprive one of the ability to see the star.

Prayers

The saying of prayers continues even in the high stages of meditation. Even though those who specialize and stress prayers, do not stress meditation, those who meditate must also say prayers. Repetitive chanting is different to strong appeals in saying prayers. And the chanting of prayers which is meant to invoke divine people is also a different form of prayer.

Meditative prayers vary, but there are two major types, those through which a divine presence is contacted and those through which a request is made. In purified meditation, however, one does not beg for petty favors, but rather for the big favor of purificatory techniques. In a sense, those who beg for petty favors such as bodily health, money and influence are not as demanding as those who beg for purificatory methods.

A man I used to know got into a money crisis. He was in bad need of money. He prayed and prayed, considered and considered, but found no relief. He worried and worried, bothered each and every one of his friends. Still he found no peace. He got some money from one man. He got some more from another. After each contribution, he found that he was still in need. He was like a hungry child who ate and ate and ate, and still remained discontent, miserable, and skinny. When he came to me, I said, "What is the problem here? You, an ant, and me, a tiny beetle. Brother, why are we asking God for money? What do we need? Can we not be happy; you with your grain of sugar and me with a tiny leaf? Are you suggesting that you need a shipment of sugar? Are you saying that I need a forest of leaves? Let us forget the desire."

When he realized what I said, he became sad. He thought I did not understand his needs.

Another person I knew, wanted to change the whole world. He perceived many defects in human society. To his mind, someone did a wrong and someone else did another wrong. He concluded that the world was ruined. When he came to me, I said, "What is it to you or to me? What have we to do with the person or power which gave the violent ones facility? Let us not worry ourselves into a mental asylum. Let us work instead for self-realization."

The main purpose of meditative prayer is to make a contact with the supernatural or divine people. It is not to beg for something. The contact itself is fulfilling.

If you say meditative prayers, always check to see if you are focused. If you are not focused while saying a prayer, repeat it and check again to see if you are focused. If you are still not focused, repeat it and check again.

Prosperity and Poverty

On one level of realization, one develops an enthusiasm to teach but if one keeps progressing, he transcends that stage. If again he falls back to human concerns, he again teaches. Fulfilling that, he advances again.

Ultimately if an ascetic is to be liberated from material social concerns, he must give up the interest in human affairs. As a man must give up his interest in the world, at least physically, when he loses his body, so an ascetic gives up the social interest eventually. And it is not that he is missed by the world. The world proceeds. The social energies keep working. The embodied beings keep fidgeting.

For promoting material existence, the soul ruins the psyche. That is the gist of it. The cycle of activity is one of ruination, progression, and ruination, alternately. Some time ago, we learned a lesson about this developing and deteriorating aspect of material nature. We lived in an area which was the habitat of some large ground lizards. These lizards grew to be three feet long. Twice during the year, these lizards flourished. They would become very happy, crawling about, running about, eating fruits, roots, catching shellfish, and whatever they could gobble down. However, twice during the year, their population dwindled.

In the same habitat there were five-foot boa constrictor snakes. The reptiles would routinely tour the area and eat every careless lizard. After an area became scarce of ground lizards, the snakes would move to other locales where other careless creatures flourished.

In turn, when the snakes flourished by eating the lizards, there would be a scarcity of food for the snakes. Then they risked their lives to eat domestic chickens. Of course that was their mistake, for then their human adversaries would shoot, chop or club them. In this way, we saw the cycle of material existence, where there is prosperity and poverty.

It is the same cycle with pious and impious activity. In one life, I became pious by good behavior. From this I developed a pious destiny. Material nature then facilitated me with fame and glory. From this fame and glory which is a sort of nourishment, I became arrogant. From that, I performed impious acts. Acting recklessly, I ruined myself. Feeling dissatisfied with the ruination, I again worked for piety. Then I again became popular. Again I became fallen. Again I strove for piety, in an endless cycle of nourishment by pious acts and degradation by impiety.

Linking the Intellect

Swāmī Shivananda taught me a technique of getting away from the calculative intelligence. So long as we are dominated either by the calculative intelligence or by the emotional life force, we will continue to miscalculate and to act irresponsibly. The intellect is a wonderful tool but it is resistant to will power. The emotions are nice but they are misleading. *Swāmī* Shivananda discussed the necessity for an ascetic to link the intellect with the purified life energy. He said:

"The two energies of intellect and life force continually interact, but generally the life force is impure. The mind compartment is not the problem. The life energy which enters the mind is the actual cause of impurity. Improve the quality of that energy by repeatedly flushing out the used, contaminated energy and taking in cleaner sensual force.

"Once a cleaner energy is ingested, bring it to the intellect or take the intellect to it. In samādhi consciousness, a pure form of the life energy is brought in contact with the intellect. Then the old ideas of material existence fade away.

"It is essential," he said, "to stop wasting energy on intellectual vices. Restrain the life force from using the intellect to pursue excessive reading, excessive thinking, gossipy conversations, and the various random expressions of speech. These drain away energy and cause the life force to be weakened."

Life Energy Distribution

Hunt for Sensations

The perpetual hunt for sensation must be given up. It is this hunt for sensation which motivates the pursuit of vices and excitements. We are dead scared of monotony, even the monotony of steady, calm consciousness. We hunt, instead, for sensation. Sensation is merely activated life energy. Sensation is an inferior way to pursue happiness.

Chapter 14

Thought Concentration

If you want to discover how much of a scatter-brain you really are, take a course in thought concentration. If you cannot take such a course, because there is no teacher in your vicinity, then try to concentrate on one thought and carefully count the number of times you are disturbed in one single period. A minute lasts 60 seconds. Still, in that period, how much of your focus shifted from or was jarred loose from a selected thought or focus?

I practiced meditation for years. I have some expertise, as these books indicate. Still, I am jarred loose in meditation.

Scatter-Brain?

Who did I intend to insult? Nobody besides myself, of course. After years of practice, a tiny thought that has no importance whatsoever, jarred me loose from the object of concentration. Someone asked: "What was the object of concentration?" I replied, "In terms of concentration, the selected object matters little, whether it is spiritual or physical. Until one reaches a level whereby one cannot be reached by thoughts, one is jarred loose."

Here is why: At the present time, with the material, subtle and causal forms, the spirit clings to the object of focus through one or two clinging tools, namely, the intellect and the life energy. Either of these can be jarred loose by thoughts. Only when these are shifted to a level beyond thought sensitivity are they unaffected by thoughts.

Thought Proneness

To get thoughts under control, one should strive to eliminate thought proneness. This means eliminating the impulsive sensitivity to thinking, and to the reception of thinking. We do not realize the quantity of psychic energy expended in thinking. How can this be curtailed? What is the value of that psychic energy which we dole out moment after moment in non-productive fantasies?

A friend of mine was so prone to thoughts, either his or someone else's, that he lived in a state of constant anxiety over fantasy thinking. He tried to analyze every thought and tried to make sense of thoughts which had no practical application. Still he claimed to enjoy himself within the mind. He was, in fact, constantly fatiguing himself. He damaged and deformed the intellect.

Usually we do not realize that the intellect is actually an organ of the subtle body just as the brain is a specific limited part of the gross form. I came to realize this, when by the grace of the great yogi, Yogeshwarananda Yogiraj, I saw my intellect visually. It was white, of an opaque hue, but shining. It had the form of a subtle, sticky sea creature like a jelly fish.

This intellect is culturally and racially biased. Until we can remove its prejudices we cannot make progress in mind and thought control. Since the intellect is polarized, it calculates how to achieve what it likes and how to avoid what it dislikes. These operations cause it to be in constant anxiety. It flashes from one sense organ to the next, trying to escape unfavorable items and to perpetuate preferred ones.

The intellect cannot be trusted since it instinctively analyzes everything it encounters. In addition it blindly serves the instincts for survival.

The two energies, the intellect and life energy, work to drain off every bit of psychic energy, but this automatic operation is unsatisfactory. So long as we endeavor to enjoy every bit of this earthly existence or of the subtle existence hereafter, we cannot understand the relationship between ourselves, the intellect, the life energy and the senses.

My suggestion is this: By analysis, the intellect develops a greater power to influence the soul. It shares that increased power with the senses for exploitation of the inner and outer world, but it does so at the soul's expense. Curb the intellect by restricting its analysis. Do not allow it to analyze everything it encounters. Restrict the analysis to things which give spiritual progression.

Flickering Intellect

Yogeshwarananda Yogiraj showed me the flickering intellect. I used to think that the *lalāta* cakra was a separate light but he showed that it is a part of the flickering intellect.

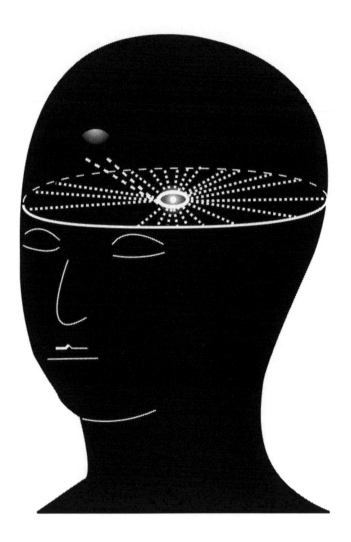

When the intellect flickers in the forehead, it is experienced as the *lalāta* cakra, which is positioned like a miner's light and which flickers with a bright white flash, off and on, off and on.

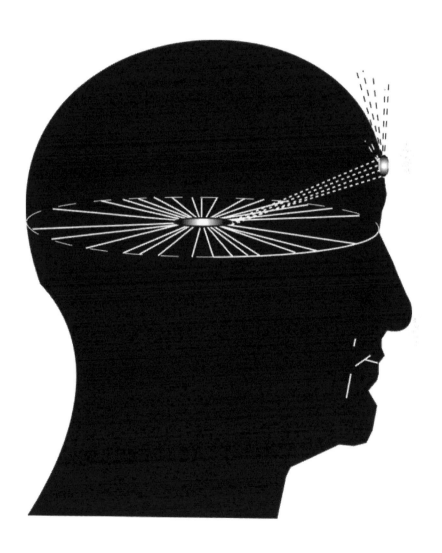

The intellect flickers to pick up sensations in the astral brain. The sensations are emitted from five pick-up points, which lead to each of the five senses.

Cross section of astral brain and sensual orbs.

These orbs orbit in a random fashion determined by the sense objects which are desired, anticipated and perceived.

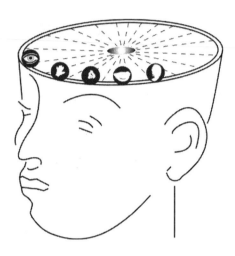

Sense control areas of the brain

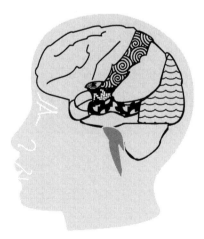

If left alone, and in most of us it is left alone, the intellect spins independently at a fast rate, sensing and interpreting thoughts and impressions. If it finds a particular impression to be worthy of exploitation, it lingers at the sensor which transmitted the impression. As soon as another excitement is sensed, it swings to absorb that. This goes on automatically without deliberation. It is based on prejudices which the intellect acquired in many, many lifetimes.

Even though we change gross bodies frequently, we retain the same subtle form with the same subtle organs like the intellect. The subtle form has acquired many prejudices which are based on rooted tendencies.

The intellect is also sensitive to the life force which functions in the body through involuntary nerves. Any time the life force prompts it or sends a signal to it, the intellect, like a dutiful servant, responds immediately. In this way the intellect is busy like a police department in a crime-prone city. All of this takes place to our detriment in terms of causing anxiety. This automatic response of the intellect fatigues us constantly. Most of all, it jars us loose from spiritual objectives. One verse comes to mind:

- *The tongue attracts the person to one pursuit, and thirst to another. The sex impulse draws him somewhere else, and the touching impulse, stomach and ears to other features. The smelling sense attracts him to another objective; the roving eyes elsewhere, and the working tendency to another aspect, just like many wives who distract a householder. (Uddhava Gītā 4.27) (Śrīmad Bhagavatam 11.9.27)*

The intellect can be curbed somewhat just by trying to improve character traits but thorough control is not attained in that way. One has to increase the purity of the energy used to spin the subtle organs. This can only be done by energizing the subtle body. Character improvement, in terms of striving to live up to the moral principles, can only take one so far.

The Yoga Process

Moral restrictions such as not lusting after another man's wife or another woman's husband, not stealing, telling the truth, or other rules of social behavior, fall under the category of *yama*. Even though such principles are considered to be the foundation of religious life, they are only the first step in this practice.

Yoga has come to mean ā*sana* postures and specialized *kriyā* actions which yield purification of the subtle body, but the broader, more complete definition of yoga consists of eight procedures: *yama, niyama, āsana,* *prāṇāyāma, pratyāhāra, dhāranā, dhyāna,* and *samādhi.* These together are the complete process.

Āsana postures have come to mean yoga because without *asana* one cannot move beyond primitive effort for *yama* and *niyama. Yama* and *niyama* are the beginning and almost all seekers agree to follow these two processes, but very few move beyond these. Under the pretext of having done elementary yoga in past lives, some others bypass *āsana* postures and *prāṇāyāma.* They view these austerities as being unnecessary. Such excuses are manifestations of laziness only, for in the current life, the subtle body is re-contaminated and it can only be partially purified without *asana* and *prāṇāyāma.*

A general listing of *yama* or moral principles is: non-violence, no untruthfulness, no stealing, no undue attachment, no pride in immoral acts, no inordinate possessiveness, no lack of faith in God, no illicit sexual indulgence, no lack of determination in spiritual discipline, no impatience towards destiny, no undue fear, no overeating, and no uncleanliness.

The practice of these principles is the beginning of religion, but some consider this to be the completion of religion.

While the moral principles *(yama)* usually concern what we ought not do, the observances or values *(niyama)* stipulate what we should do. These are: perform austerity, cultivate an attitude of contentment, put faith in God and the scriptures, routinely worship God, be knowledgeable of material nature, the spirits and the Supreme spirit, recite sacred hymns, behave modestly and perform traditional worship ceremonies. Thus *yama* and *niyama* mean what should not be done and what should be done for the development of character in the social world.

However, for an in-depth spirituality, a human being will have to purify the inner nature. This deals with the root of the problems. The next step is *āsana* postures which deal with trying to get the gross body under control, to bring it into a state of efficiency whereby the least-possible amount of energy is used in its maintenance. This conservation of energy causes an increase in psychic perception, something that is necessary for achievement of psychic purity.

After being proficient in *āsana* postures, one naturally advances to prāṇāyāma, since *prana* is the subtle fluid in the subtle body. To get that psychic form under control, to purify it, one takes up prāṇāyāma. Once this is achieved, the next step is *pratyāhāra,* which is to retract the sensual energies.

In material existence, these energies are constantly going outwards in the search for matching external enjoyment. This outward-going tendency causes a dispersion of attention which reduces self-focus. Thus, once the gross body is somewhat purified, the subtle form is brought under control by drawing in subtle energies. If one completes the *pratyāhāra* retraction of sensual energy, one gets experiences of soul power. One begins to understand the spirit self. Thereafter one takes to *dhāranā* concentration, which is controlled focus of the conserved sensual force.

It requires many years of practice, to develop these skills. One needs expert guidance, great patience and individual instruction. Each person requires individual instruction that is tailored for the removal of unique impurities.

The final two steps in the yoga system, those of *dhyāna* effortless linkage of attention, and *samādhi* continuous effortless linkage of attention, are attempted at all stages, but these only fructify in the advanced practice, after one mastered the elementary disciplines.

My advice is this: Start where you are. Begin with a discipline that comes naturally to you. Select part of the process that makes sense to you. Do not allow yourself to become stagnant at the starting point. If *āsana* and *prāṇāyāma* are too difficult, or if you feel that these are unnecessary, then proceed as you are. Just do not allow yourself to stagnate. Do not be afraid to advance to a higher stage if your present view changes. As you improve, some of your opinions will be altered. Adjust yourself as you progress.

Determination

One's determination is regularly broken in spiritual life. People take vows as if they can follow these without deviation but actually no one can guarantee that a vow may not be ruptured. We are not that absolute. Still we should take vows, for that might be the only way to maintain a partial sense of honor; the only way to make a repeated effort of reform.

Even though we should take vows, we should also be humble towards providence, for at any time, it might force any of us to deviate. Many ascetics who take vows of celibacy are forced to overlook their pledges. Why laugh at or criticize that? Even religious householders break the vow for restricted sexual indulgence.

I am one person who was not able to maintain the householder vows until I took up yoga and achieved some success at certain technical *kriyās*. And even then, I found that I broke the vows in the subtle body. My gross body became reformed, but my subtle form remained as lusty as ever. Still, I meet many others who speak of strict vows. I am appalled at their vast ignorance of our subtle deviant activities.

They have no idea of the sexual contact we make through the subtle body. Despite the show of faith on the physical side, we do not have sufficient subtle perception to know the impulsions which overtake us on the subtle side.

Determination is good. Where would any of us be without it? Nevertheless, one's determination is repeatedly jarred from the objectives by the moving force of the thoughts of others. Have you ever observed that even though you become determined, another unrelated idea pops into your head to successfully divert you from the original intention? We are continually assaulted, carried away, by thoughts which pop into the mind. How can we control this?

All forms of concentration are broken by incoming thoughts. It is not the method of concentration that is being discussed, for all forms of concentration used by disciplinary seekers are broken, interrupted, and disrupted by incoming thoughts. Thus the necessity exists to put the mind out of touch with such incoming vibrations. I tried several forms of concentration and found that in all cases, thoughts jar me away from the selected sound, idea, or object. Only when the mind and spirit are at a considerable psychic distance from the realm of disturbing thoughts, am I able to pursue the selected focus without interruption.

Here is an example: I typed this sentence at 1 o'clock in the early morning, an hour after midnight. For a limited period of time, a married woman tried to reach me by thought. Her husband was a semi-religious man. She was a semi-religious lady. Somehow, she tried to contact me mentally each morning. I had not heard from her for about three weeks. Then, all of a sudden, I saw her mind trying to reach mine.

How can she reach me? I will explain:

She heard from someone that I rose early as a matter of course. Since she got the information she tried to contact me even if her physical body was sleeping. She made it her duty to interrupt me in the wee hours of the morning. Even though she did not rise that early for devotions, disciplines, or anything else, she broke my concentration by thought projection.

Whose fault is it? It is my fault only.

I informed someone of my early rising. That news spread to my detriment. On some mornings I anticipated that she would contact me, so I hid in the thought world. Then I saw her thoughts travelling, trying to locate my mind to discharge energy. If I failed to dodge thought, if it made contact, I saw her smile with satisfaction in her sleep, as if to say, "There! Right on target! I affected him. His meditation was shattered." If the thought failed to locate me, it pursued the search for awhile, then it lost power and disappeared.

One early morning as I sat to meditate, some religious friends wanted to reach me. They were sleeping physically but they congregated in the astral world near their sleeping bodies. They thought of me. One of them said, "What do you think he is doing?" Another one said, "I bet he is up doing yoga. The guy is crazy. He feels he must get up that early for religious life and austerities. I feel it is unnecessary. Let us go and see if he is awake. Some yogis fool others and say that they rise early while in fact, they sleep soundly."

As they discussed this, the thoughts came to me. The psychic energies broke my concentration. Since the thoughts concerned me, I had to accept the vibrations. In that case, these friends got too much information about me and so I was distracted because they knew my schedule.

Enjoyable Thoughts

Some thoughts are enjoyable. Others are disliked by the receiver. Usually as soon as a thought comes into the mind, it is instantly checked by the intellect for enjoyable content. If it has none, the intellect analyzes it anyway. This is the defect of the intellect. It analyzes any and every thought, sensation, impression, surface, sound, shape, smell or taste it encounters. Due to this defect we suffer from undue attachment. Attachment is a hazard to spiritual life. There is a discipline in yoga practice just for ridding a person of attachment. However, one cannot develop perfect detachment merely by assuming a detached mood. For perfect detachment one has to elevate the life energy and provide the intellect with a higher level of operational energy.

Let us take the example of a jet engine. It cannot operate efficiently if it does not have a high octane fuel. It does not matter what the technician does; if the fuel is of a poor grade, the engine cannot work properly. If the life energy is not of a very high grade, an ascetic cannot achieve success in detachment. He may exhibit detachment periodically, but he cannot do so consistently.

When an enjoyable thought comes, the intellect does not try to reject it, but instead tries to enjoy it even more. It is just like a hungry child. If the baby is hungry and you put the mother's breast to the infant's mouth, the child will suck and suck until the breast no longer has milk or fluffiness. Then the child will suck on the nipple for a few more times and reject the nipple in disgust, as if to say, "Where is the milk? What about that nice fluffy feeling?"

Due to this enjoying mentality, the intellect is a setback in spiritual life. Because it usually operates on its own, the intellect is difficult to curb.

Since the intellect wants to enjoy, it is attracted to enjoyable vices. This is its defect. As soon as the intellect tries to escape from a vice, it becomes trapped by the pleasure it derived.

I will give an example. I used to be with this group of spiritual seekers. I joined to get a particular technique. However, they did not want to give the technique without charging the price of one year of service to their teacher. This was a very high price. I needed the technique badly. I could not find any other group in the vicinity who knew it. Thus I made a decision to pay the one year service.

I began the service. As it worked out, the leading disciple of that teacher suspected that I was not willing to become a yes-man of the group. He deliberately assigned me a menial service. Thereafter in the astral world, some of the female followers invited me to a religious party. This was not on the physical level. These parties occurred on the astral side only. They had a reputation for observing religious principles. They took no chances doing anything that would have smeared their fame on the physical side. When I got to the party, I saw the leading disciple and some other male persons with some of the females, all involved in sexual affairs.

I sat down and pretended that I was at ease and that what they were doing was in order. Even though I was in the astral world, I knew well that this hypocrisy was harmful to our spiritual life but I had no choice but to toe the line since I needed a valuable technique introduced by their teacher.

Sensing that I felt something was wrong, the leading disciple left the party with one of the females. Later, this same young lady came to me and began to flirt. In the astral world, she was nude. Her husband, who was nearby with another woman, was nude as well. To decrease the suspicion, I removed my shirt but retained a covering below my waist. I began to talk to her. Then I said, "I will have to go now because I have to wake my body on the other side to attend duties. If I am late the service will be neglected." She replied, "Hey, cool off! Everything is alright. The chief disciple is here with us. He arranged this party. I am supposed to break you in. Do you not like me? Let us get on with it." But I said, "I must complete the services. Do not take it personally. I enjoy your company but I must fulfill the assigned duties."

At this point the girl smiled and started to touch and rub her body on mine. To escape her, I began to rub her body to reciprocate. As soon as I began, her intellect began to enjoy the pleasure energies. She could not keep vigilance. Her determination to keep me shattered. She began to enjoy some more and I suddenly escaped and awoke my gross body.

It is not that this is unusual. This can happen to anyone. Even if the activity is against our desire, it may carry us away if the intellect locates a tiny bit of enjoyment. Here is a quote:

- *When the mind is prompted by the wandering senses, it utilizes the discernment, just as in water, the wind handles a ship. (Bhagavad Gītā 2.67)*

In the days before birth control pills and other means of pregnancy prevention, many women became pregnant against their will merely because they could not utilize their intellect discriminately while enjoying sexual contact. By the same token, many men begot children whimsically merely because they could not stop the life energy from emitting itself while enjoying romantically. In either case, the factor of enjoyment contributed to an undesirable result.

Unpalatable thoughts, the ones we dislike, help us considerably. These alert the intellect to stop the effort at enjoyment, but the enjoyable thoughts act as an enticement. This causes the development of attachment to what is unwanted.

The Pleasure Need

Since we crave pleasure and cannot keep away from it, we are trapped in the use of the intellect for analyzing the pleasurable content of thoughts. We run from a blank mind which we consider dull and boring. We try to discover whatever is enjoyable in the incoming thoughts. This tendency contributes to indetermination.

To understand our position we may consider a woman who recently delivered a baby. The factors of morning sickness during the early pregnancy, the discomfort of carrying the weighty fetus during the later months, the anxiety regarding the onset of labor, the labor pains themselves, the stretching of the lower abdomen, the stretching of the birthing passage, the pain of it all, the delivery of the child, the soreness of the organ after delivery, the precautions given by the doctor or midwife and the anxiety for the security of the child, all these should, by due reason, serve to invoke sexual restraint. Still, even before the sexual organ heals, it requires more sexual entries.

Thought Energy in the Mind

One should observe how thought energy comes into the mind, is detected by the flashing intellect, is processed and then subsides. As I said previously, the intellect is an organ in the subtle body just as any gland is an organ in the gross form. If one cannot realize or see this organ, one can still detect the mind space which the intellect inhabits. One can observe how one becomes aware of thoughts, either as ideas, subtle sounds, or pictures. One can notice how the intelligence or calculative mental energy responds to incoming thoughts, how these are usually processed, and how gradually, even the most intense thought subsides into nothingness or is stored in the subconscious as a troublesome or treasured memory. One can understand the lack of resistance to undesirable thoughts which one does not have the power to reject outright or which remain in the mind despite efforts to eject them. Whether one chants or meditates, still, some undesirable thoughts are so powerful and make such a mark within the consciousness, that they remain in the mind no matter what a person may do to eliminate them.

Thinking / Electric Power

Normally we have little need to conserve thinking power. Since we are grossly oriented we think in terms of either conserving, utilizing or wasting gross energy. We care little about thinking force. At some stage, however, one must realize that thoughts are a more valuable energy. We waste vast amounts of thinking power and exhaust ourselves mentally without even realizing it.

Here is the reason: The wastage of thinking energy usually goes unnoticed. It decreases the quality of mind energy. It causes an increase in haphazard thinking activity.

Concentration

The subject of concentration becomes important when we try to withdraw ourselves from the external world. If we successfully withdraw sensual energies from external interests by slowing or stopping the outward flow of those energies from the psyche, then we are immediately faced with another problem, that of how and where to concentrate the energies.

If, for instance, an engineer stops the flow of a stream, he will be faced with the problem of where to conserve the water. Obviously, if one dams a stream without making room for the conserved water, it will seek a reservoir on its own. This happens when we develop sensual restraint. Thus, in the eight-part yoga process, one has to master directive concentration just after applying sensual restraint. In Sanskrit, sensual restraint is known as *pratyāhāra* and directive concentration is known as *dhāranā*.

Some say that it is better not to attempt sensual restraint. They feel that if the energy is held in check, it will flow unrestrictedly through another avenue of expression. For instance, if a seeker restrains sexually, and is not prepared for hormone containment, he might become haughty and politically-minded. The energy which he conserved from the sexual usages converts into political drive for social power.

This occurs because of ignoring the eight-part process of yoga and by taking shelter of teachers who did not perfectly master every phase of yoga. One must, if he conserves power from one area, concentrate it in another area; otherwise one will be forced into another direction impulsively, just as a river would divert itself in an easy direction if its flow is blocked by a dam.

The teacher is supposed to be an expert at psychological disciplines. When he tells the disciple to conserve sexual power, he should also advise where the disciple should store or utilize that reserved energy. In fact, a particular type of conserved power is to be stored in a particular way. A general instruction is useless as a technique. Even though all rivers will swell upstream if their courses are blocked, each requires a particular type of reservoir and a particular type of flood outlet. Each meditator has a particular hang-up or vice-proneness and must be advised individually.

In my case as a teacher, I have some experience in the conservation of sexual power, but only in relation to channeling the conserved power into responsible householder life which entails caring for a family. Otherwise I have no practical experience. Suppose a celibate monk comes to me. He may inquire, "I heard that you are proficient in celibacy. I am having difficulty with containment. What should I do? How can I channel this energy?"

Then, what should I say? Should I con him, fool him, and pretend to have a practical method. As a *sannyāsī*, he cannot use the method of channeling I used. He needs a different method because he took a vow not to have a family. In other words, I could be compared to an engineer who dammed a river to create a hydroelectric plant. But if another engineer comes to me who wants to operate an irrigation system, I cannot advise him practically. Both of us are interested in water conservation but our usage of the energy is different. A senior engineer who is experienced in both types of application of water power can advise either of us. But he must have practical experience, not just a big name, some charisma and a prestigious organization.

Typically, in the yoga system, when one first retracts the sensual powers, one is advised to concentrate on some point within the physical and subtle body, since presently, in any living body, the two forms are interlocked. After one conserves the energy within the body, one is advised to focus it on an energy junction or on the core-self.

In the example of the use of river power for hydroelectric generation, the engineer cannot get electricity merely by stopping the flow of the water. He must build a generator. It is the same with the sensual power. This is why one is told in yoga to focus on chakras or on other key points within the subtle body.

Places for Concentration

There are many places for concentration within the gross and subtle bodies. Usually beginners are asked by yoga teachers to focus the mind between the eyebrows. This is mentioned in the Bhagavad Gītā:

- *Excluding the external sensual contacts, and fixing the visual focus between the eyebrows, putting the inhalation and exhalation in balance, moving through the nose,*
- *...the wise man, who is dedicated to achieving liberation, whose sensual energy, mind and intellect are controlled, whose desire, fear and anger are gone, is liberated always. (Bhagavad Gītā 5.27-28)*

Furthermore, the other concentration points which are called chakras or energy-gyrating centers, are discussed by Lord Krishna when He instructed Uddhava. It was explained by Lord Shiva when He instructed *Nārada* in the *Nārada Pañcaratra*. Thus these are standard, approved locations for internal concentration within the body.

- *Blocking the anus with the heel, and lifting the vital energy to the heart chakra, then through the chest, throat and head, and by taking it through the hole at the top of the head of the subtle body, one should transfer to the spiritual existence, while giving up the gross form. (Uddhava Gītā 10.24) (Śrīmad Bhagavatam 11.15.24)*

In trying to escape from penetrating thoughts, one may find it necessary to shift from the brain area. This part of the body acts as a sensitive radio because the intellect of the subtle body is interspaced there. The mind is the brain of the subtle form. It detects incoming thoughts and reacts impulsively.

In trying to master concentration, one discovers that some thoughts are resistant to will power. Some carry a penetrating potency whereby they remain in the mind, even if they are undesirable. Thus one may switch out of the brain area and dodge such irritating ideas. Instead of fighting off such thoughts mentally, one may switch to a lower chakra such as the base of the spine. That is the lowest of the energy-gyrating centers on the spinal column. That is a no-thought location. At that location, the intellect cannot sense thoughts, nor can it act or react to ideas. In the beginning one may turn the entire subtle body upside-down within the gross one, bringing the intellect and core-self into the base chakra region of the gross body.

One may practice this in stages, mastering one technique after the other:

1st Technique

Practice meditating on the centralized core-self. As soon as one feels centered, shift the focus to the base of the spine

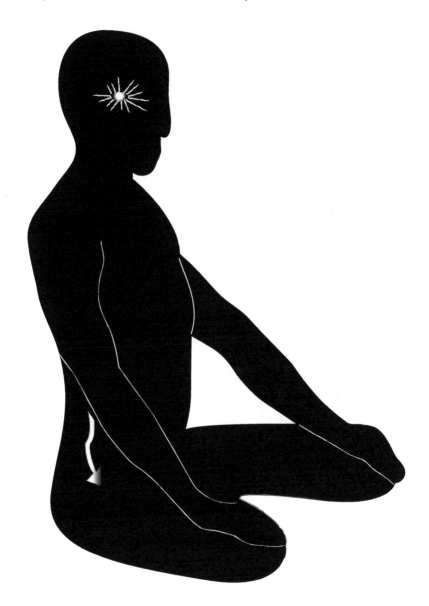

2nd *Technique*

After mastering the previous practice, make efforts to shift the focal core-self to the base of the spine. Be patient with yourself during this practice. Do not be hasty. Do not expect instant success.

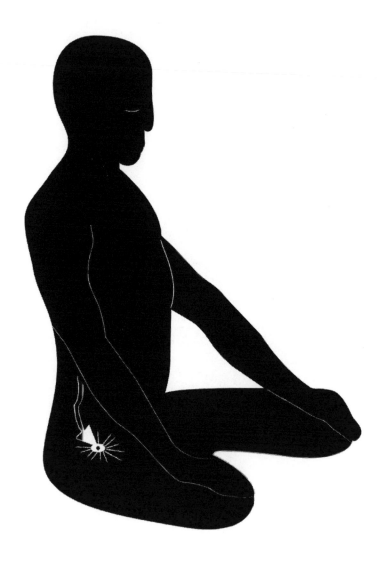

3rd Technique

Detect the subtle body which is interspaced in the gross one. Remain as still as possible.

4th Technique

Detect the subtle body as well as the core-self.

5th _Technique_

Detect the subtle body, core-self and base chakra.

6th Technique

Flip the subtle body, so that the core-self remains centralized in the head of the subtle form, while the base chakra remains in the gross form.

In material existence, the base chakra remains stationed in the base chakra of the gross form, even when the subtle body is separated from it temporarily. When the subtle body is permanently separated from the gross form, the life force shifts fully into the subtle form.

7th Technique

After the 6th technique is achieved, one may keep the subtle body upright, aligned with the gross one, and relocate only the core-self and intellect.

Let the subtle body remain in its normal position in the gross form. Move the core-self to the base chakra.

Meditation Practice

Unless concentration is mastered, and unless disturbing thoughts are left untouched, one cannot meditate. This should not discourage meditation attempts. The most confused, most neurotic person can meditate but he will have little success. As soon as one tries to meditate, one discovers the mind content and realizes that one must do battle with thoughts, ideas, impressions and imaginings. The meditation begins only when the ascetic can concentrate without mental interruptions.

One should conserve all sensual energy, concentrate at approved points in the body, simmer down and transfer the self to a higher level where it is out of reach of incoming thoughts. If one fails to do this, the meditation is a struggle only.

The subtle energy or *prana* is the sensual power. Unless this energy is calmed and stabilized, one cannot meditate. However, even if one cannot meditate, one can conserve and concentrate the psychological powers. When attempting to meditate, most people are either restraining, concentrating, relaxing or enjoying sensual energy. Usually they do not complete either the process of conservation or concentration, because the intellect keeps detecting and responding to incoming thoughts, an action which frustrates the effort.

I learned some intellect-stabilizing techniques from a few yogis. And until I learned these, I could not meditate. I also learned how to get purified pranic energy in the subtle body, for without this, the intellect does not settle down and does not lose its interest in the external reactionary world.

If you want to meditate in earnest, then you are required to do this much:

- *Be isolated.*
- *Have time to practice.*
- *Be free of social involvements.*

The Critical Nature

One aspect of thought is critical analysis. Every person has a critical tendency. It is natural. Some make more use of it, but each has it. I found that so long as the life energy is not energized, the intellectual mechanism for critical thinking continues its involvements on lower levels to my detriment.

Dreams

For more remembrance of dreams, many precautions need be taken. But why take precautions if dreams have little importance? The reason is this: Dreams have great importance to one who wants success in spiritual life. For now, dreams are a way of judging how one applies moral values in the subtle world. It is a way of knowing how we will perform in the hereafter.

A small aspect, such as holding urine in the body during resting or sleeping, contributes to reduced remembrance of dreams. It is not that urination is directly related to memory. Rather, urination is sponsored by the same energy which activates memory. If retention of urine takes some of the energy, less of it is made available for activating memory.

In the case of a man's income, part of it is used for sanitation, part for religion and part for education. If the sanitation cost increases, the amount allotted to religion and education will, in effect, decrease. Thus a reduction in the expenses for sanitation causes an increase in other areas.

Both the holding of stool and that of urine causes a reduction in psychic perception. We should promptly evacuate stools and expel urine. Before retiring at night, we can make one last call to empty the bladder and bowels. During the night if we feel the urge, we can give up the lazy attitude, get up and do the needful. It is worth the effort.

After careful observation, I can say this: Any small amount of urine or stool retained, causes an increase in sleep requirement, an increase in drowsiness, and a decrease in psychic awareness. It causes one to have less-enlightening dreams and more lower association in the subtle world.

To reduce the need for evacuation or urine expulsion during sleep, one can regulate the times for eating and drinking. It is easier to control the times of drinking than the times of eating. For example, one may stop taking liquids just before bed time or at least one hour before bed time. Any liquid taken at bed time will be processed through the kidneys while the body rests. Urine will be stored in the bladder and such storage requires the use of vital energy which could, instead, be used for increased dream recall.

Dreams and Hypocrisy

Dreams helped me to understand hypocrisy. Once I got control over physical sexual desire, I was still faced with a lack of subtle control. I found that even though I was reformed on the physical level, I broke the celibate aims in dreams. But a person might say, "It is just a dream. It is not real."

Actually, it is just as realistic as the physical plane. By these dreams, I was shown that I would fail the test for celibacy if I were to pass away from the physical body. Dreams are meaningful. They show an ascetic where he fails, where his austerity falls short of the standard.

Some years ago I was attracted to a married lady. I knew her husband. In any case, because of morality on this gross level, I could not act out the attraction. The lady was similarly attracted. Even though we both raked and scraped our brains, neither of us could find a way to fulfill the sexual attraction. At the time, I began to understand clearly that we were being prompted by body-needing souls in the hereafter. Regardless, the realization did not dispel the attraction.

As it turned out, I moved away from the area, and as it is said: *Out of sight, out of mind.* Since I did not see the lady I forgot the attraction. But there is another saying: *Absence makes the heart grow fonder.* Thus by that, I used to meet the lady in dreams about every nine months. After these dreams, I would clearly remember what transpired. I drew the conclusion that our mutual attraction was due to desire and association in a past life.

Gradually by the grace of Shiva, I began to understand that this association was detrimental to my celibate aims. Still, I could not stop the dreams. Every nine months or so, I found myself in the association of that lady, pursuing the romance. Some time in 1996, I had one particular dream with the lady, when I saw Ganesha, the deity with elephant features. When I saw him, I made no attempt to greet him. After the dream was concluded, I returned to my physical body. Then I meditated to reach Ganesha. Fortunately, he did not ignore me. He came. I then said, "What trick is this? You supernatural people know of my desire to be a perfect celibate. If you arrange for me to meet this lady every so often and to meet the subtle bodies of other women, what will happen to my celibate aims?"

He replied, "Nobody is at fault for this. It is your nature that causes this. Why blame others? You saw me when you were involved with the breezy affections of a woman from your past life, but what have I to do with it? I am just a checker. I have to make sure that emotional tensions are satisfactorily resolved. Why blame me for this?

"Whatever you began in the past life, continues in the present time. Who else but you is responsible for this? Unless you are a Buddha, how can you stop this?"

Some time after, I again met the woman in the subtle world. Somehow, by this instruction of deity Ganesha, I stopped the romance in the mid-part of that meeting. Unlike Buddha. I cannot abruptly cut off material existence. But if I am serious enough, if I make it a priority, slowly and surely I can end the hypocrisy.

I have traced my fate with this particular woman to the following forces:

- *a previous desire to be with her in a past life*
- *a natural attraction to her whereby any time I encounter her in any world anywhere, I am attracted*
- *the charismatic force of the woman's nature*
- *another ascetic's frustration with not being able to control this woman*

Let me explain this in detail.

The previous desire which is being rekindled in this life can be eliminated by seeing the impracticality of it and by realizing that there is nothing special in it. It is inappropriate. Destiny does not endorse it. I can oppose destiny but that would be futile. Even if destiny permits, destiny itself will destroy it in the end. No purpose is served in opposing destiny. Nothing except frustration would be gained.

The natural attraction between me and the lady is a case of matching life energies. By nature, the woman has some energy which compliments mine. The flaw in such matching energies is this: It is not a complete match. Only part of her energies matches mine. The unmatched parts would cause conflicts sooner or later. The matching energies should not be taken seriously.

Within those matching energies is an allowance for generating progeny on the physical plane. But what is that for me? That means more responsibility for infant forms. The entities who might use such bodies may not appreciate me, even if I were to marry this woman in this or some other life. It would be foolish for me to think that by reproducing, I would gain fulfillment in a parental role. There is absolutely nothing in it. All the entities who are parented are parents themselves. They will assume adult forms periodically. Thus the whole range of parenting, though necessary and useful on the physical level, is in fact, a great pretense.

Only very foolish entities take such a thing seriously. Parenting has to be done. It should be done but that does not mean that it is a spiritual duty. It is merely a social routine, carried out by humans and animals alike. Even insects serve as parents. What is so special about it? Something that is necessary on the physical level may be irrelevant on higher planes. Thus we need not take all physical aspects seriously.

The factor of the other ascetic who was frustrated because he could not control this woman can be dealt with also. This ascetic is a hypocritical celibate monk. He has no yoga and *prāṇāyāma* techniques for celibacy and yet he allowed a teacher to flatter him with the title of monk. This ascetic used to take energy from me to attract and control this woman. Now I have stopped that transfer of energy. Even though he is a friend, if he wants the woman, he will have to endeavor honestly to get her. What have I to do with it?

This explanation shows the usefulness of dreams. Dreams do help us to recognize, and then eliminate hypocrisy.

Deviation in Dreams

Dream recall is applicable in other areas. Take, for instance, the austerity of diet. That can be broken in dreams. A deviation in austerity, may occur in any discipline. Here is an example. A friend of mine met me in a dream recently. Once before, we were members of a spiritual society. Both of us lived in the same dormitory.

Recently I met him in a dream. He began cooking his favorite potato soup. It so happened that it was late in the astral world, around 11:00 p.m. on the physical side. Still he sanctified those foods ritually, and then served them for eating. He sat down and ate immediately. I knew I could not gorge because it would affect yoga practice negatively. I slipped away from him.

Before I left, I pretended to enjoy the meal, but the little bit which entered my subtle body began to hurt that body considerably. The food he prepared was subtle food only, but he considered it as physical food. Because of lack of objectivity in dreams, he could not realize that we were in the subtle existence only.

Yoga may be practiced once, twice, thrice or more frequently per day in full or shortened sessions. Usually the early morning session, soon after rising, is the most important one. To make the best of this early morning session, one should not eat in the late afternoon or during the night.

The question is: Since yoga postures concern the physical body, why bother to restrain the astral body from subtle food? Postures concern both the physical and astral bodies simultaneously. *Prāṇāyāma* breath practice is aimed at the subtle form but *prāṇāyāma* cannot be successful if the gross body is not curbed. The gross body draws energy from the subtle form. Thus it is important to keep both bodies in the healthiest condition.

In addition, if one overeats in the astral world or eats at the wrong time, he will by the law of nature, be forced to duplicate that activity in this gross world.

Dreams and Influences from Past Lives

Many influences from a person's past life manifest in the present to haunt the self. Whatever we were involved in, carries responsibility. Still, even though we were implicated, we should handle the liabilities in a way that brings a conclusion, not an expansion and further irritation. In dreams, as well as in physical life, many persons approach for favors and services which they feel we ought to render willingly. Thus unless we are conscious in dreams, we cannot act with discrimination.

Here is an example: Recently a daughter of my present body, whose past body was my grandmother, assumed her old granny form in the astral world. She tried to get me to marry a girl I knew in childhood. The three of us met in the astral world by the force of past association. Even though I was aware of what transpired, the other two were not conscious of their psychic actions. This occurs because the subtle body can assume forms based on pressures and tensions within it. It can do this, even without the conscious knowledge of the person concerned. The subtle body is that impulsive.

Let me give more information. In the present life, when this body was ten years of age. I lived with one of my grandmothers. She knew a young girl whom she felt I should marry. It so happened that later on, at the age of thirteen, I moved from that area and did not see that grandmother or the girl again. However the desire of that grandmother was so strong, that it remained in her subtle body for some thirty years. Even though she passed on and took another physical form, still her subtle body carried that desire for me to marry the girl. The form went so far as to assume the old elderly appearance in order to assert its previous social authority. This means that tendencies in the subtle body persist, even if they assume another form.

Cross-Worlds

There are many adjacent cross-worlds which are easily accessible to us. Since their energy frequencies are just a little higher or lower than this place, they are, existentially speaking, merely a step away. Even though, for us, these locations are subtle or perhaps imaginary, the persons who live there experience these places physically. They developed suitable bodies to experience those places in a gross way.

This is not hard to understand. For us, this physical world is a cross-world when we are in the hereafter as disembodied souls requiring physical forms. Even for us, this place was dreamy, flimsy and subtle, when we first entered the emotions of our parents for developing the present gross forms. Thus it is not hard to imagine the existence of these cross-worlds. Knowledge of these places results in a decrease of attachment to this physical place.

Once I found myself in a parallel world which was very similar to this earthly place. I was drawn there by persons who had long departed material bodies and who lived in their last bodies in Guyana. Since my present body took birth there and accepted services from some of those departed persons, they developed a power to transfer my subtle form there.

As usual, when I arrived I forgot my existence over here. This forgetfulness is something I desire to eliminate. In the near future I hope to report to readers that I did indeed overcome this lack of objectivity. When I arrived into that parallel world, those persons who helped raise my body in Guyana in infancy and who passed on, wanted me to become a teacher. To their minds, I was quite suitable as a school teacher. They had no view of my ambitions for increased spiritual perception. In fact, even though I forgot the existence on this side of life, still my need for and yearning for liberation continued there.

Suddenly those persons told me that I was appointed to a school and that I would be the chief teacher. I was shocked. Not only did I forget my existence on this side, but I felt trapped on the other side in the association of those culturally-concerned people. Actually that world is just like this one. People here are also concerned primarily with cultural improvement.

In that other world, there was hardly any rudeness in the children. And combined with that, there was no intoxication or liquor-drinking habits by men. Thus from the cultural view, it was a desirable place. Still to me, it was a prison. Suddenly, just as I arrived there, I found myself withdrawn.

On April 27th of 1997, I accidentally fell asleep in a room where the ventilation was restricted. Since the air breathed through the gross form was of a poor quality, the subtle body became de-energized as soon as it left the physical form. Then it entered a cross-world.

After entering that dimension, I did, for the time being, forget my existence in this world. I noticed that the religion there was similar to the Hinduism of this world. They used a language which was similar to Hindi. There were no racial biases, but there was a disparity in the varying levels of intelligence. Some people predominated just as in this world.

There was a police force but crime was infrequent. I attended a lecture by a priest. Later on after I came back to the physical body, the Shiva Deity informed me that the priest was troublesome. He said: "I endeavored to curb him for some time."

Shiva did not explain what he meant by "some time". But later that day, knowing that I wondered about the duration, his voice echoed in my head, "It was a very, very long time, longer than you can know."

A reader may observe that while I was in the cross-world, I forgot my existence here. But as soon as I came back here, I remembered the occurrence there. This is better than going to such a place, and not remembering the transfer. Still, I should improve recall so that I can objectively know while crossing over and consciously be aware that I left a physical body behind in this place. Such knowledge would help me in preparation for the death of this physical form.

After all, for spiritual success, I should know when my material body dies. I should not be like my departed mother, who, even three months after she left her physical form, still thought that she could return to it and still made repeated efforts to awaken it, even though it was long cremated. What is the use of a religion or austerities, if one does not know objectively when one has left the physical body behind temporarily or permanently, and has gone to another world?

Oversleeping / Poor Dream Recall

Oversleeping is caused by bad association. There are other causes but these other reasons are traceable to the bad association which prevails in our lives. For instance, if I work strenuously, I might oversleep. The gross and subtle bodies will demand that I do so for rejuvenation. Strenuous work may be a consequence of bad association. Bad association is not easy to eliminate. We usually feel that bad association comes from irreligious people only. That is not true. Bad association also comes from righteous persons and from family relations. Due to having little or no dream recall, one cannot control the influences which affect one in the dream world.

Here is a method for tracking bad association. As soon as you oversleep, realize it, but do not jolt your mind away suddenly from the sleeping mood. Be conscious of it without shifting out of it abruptly. Silently and calmly, without alarm, take note of images, impressions or thoughts which are displayed in the mind. Once you note this, you should awaken the mind fully. After noting the images, impressions, thoughts or ideas, record them in a notebook. Analyze them and trace them to particular persons.

Easy as this may sound, it is a tedious process. Before you can realize that you overslept, you must first develop a habit of setting a reasonable limit for resting. If, for instance, I lie down to rest for six hours, I should have a clear idea of when to rise. I might have to use an alarm clock or ask someone to call me.

If I enjoy oversleeping, or if I feel I am entitled to it, or that it is harmless, I will be unable to analyze the dream association properly. For instance: In the case of the romantic dream, a person might recall the emotional enjoyment and sensual pleasure and even the lover. Even though the mind recalls this, it will be unable to analyze properly. The enjoyment would remove the discriminatory power, causing the intellect to malfunction.

The most difficult task is to recall non-enjoyable dreams. These, if recalled, are easier to analyze. Usually one remembers that one had an unfavorable time or one feels depressed and uncomfortable, but one does not recall the details. In some cases, hours or days after, the dream is suddenly recalled. Thus one should study the workings of the mind to find out why it has the defect of poor recall.

Deposit of Problem Energies

Prayers, even though a popular way of divine communication, can be an impediment in spiritual life. The same statement can be applied to chanting or singing. These spiritual communications which are easy and practical, are frequently misused.

I found that establishing a place of pilgrimage or establishing an altar or a Deity, can be a source of distress for an ascetic. Once these are established, it is only a matter of time before they are abused. For instance, if one has a Deity established on an altar, people may bring problems there. Once deposited, these problem-energies must be taken care of, either by the Deity or by the devotee who maintains the sacred place. Suppose the Deity does not remove the bad energy? Then what happens? Who absorbs it?

Once, years ago, in 1989, a man asked me to visit an abandoned temple in a rural village in Guyana. I hesitated to do this. The man, however, was insistent. After several pleas, I agreed to go. He was happy, but as soon as I got to the place, I began to sweat profusely. Many hereafter people, who were trapped on the other side of life and who wanted infant bodies, were at that place. As soon as they saw me, they formed a queue and began requesting release.

These hereafter folk had left physical bodies, but could not, due to twirks of destiny, get new forms. They begged me over and over to use mystic power to release them. Seeing the situation, I began to refer them to Shiva, whose lingam representation was at that place.

After touring the grounds for some time, with the friend who took me there, we found an old concrete form of a *Hanumān* deity under a peepul sacred tree. Seeing *Hanumān*, I was astonished. "How did you get here?" I asked him. "How long were you under this tree which grew through the concrete of the temple yard?"

He replied, "That is a long story. The time of my release and reinstallment is not due. Do what you can for these unlucky ghosts and then leave this place." Thus, by *Hanumān's* advice, I expended mystic energy and broke the spell that kept those spirits from getting new material bodies. They were thankful. I pointed in the direction of the *Hanumān mūrti*, and they all began bowing to him repeatedly. Their subtle forms then faded from that place. The point is: Any pilgrimage, place of worship or altar may be overloaded with problem energies. The system of prayers and other easy methods are avenues for abusage.

Any friend or devotee who refuses to or is unable to simplify his life, who has problems and who comes to see a Deity at a temple or at home, will, of necessity, leave behind negative energies. The person takes relief in seeing the Deity and automatically deposits resentments and frustrations. Such energy must be carefully handled in order to cleanse the place.

Adjusting Material Nature

One big problem is to try to adjust material nature. Unfortunately we cannot make adjustments. Thus the alternative is to adjust ourselves or to shift into another phase of existence either in relation to material nature or completely outside its unfavorable influence. Most seekers plan to change material nature to suit themselves. They go to a spiritual master or a Deity to get power to adjust nature. Some spiritual masters take advantage of such seekers. The exploitive teachers indicate that they have a method for adjustment. This is a scam. Material nature will remain as it is forever and ever. If there is any change, it will only be in ourselves. All endeavors to adjust material nature at large are futile. The practical effort is to adjust one's individual nature in terms of how it responds to material nature.

Containment of Sensual Energies

Before meditation or *dhyāna*, and before trance or *samādhi*, the yoga system has two stages: *pratyāhāra* and *dhāranā*. Unless one completes these stages, there is no question of mastering meditation and trance states. If a person masters *pratyāhāra* or containment of sensual energies and if he masters *dhāranā* or concentrated usage of his contained sensuality, he will not be baffled with suppressed tendencies.

In the case of the engineer who dams up a river, he took the first step which is *pratyāhāra*. *Pratyāhāra* means that I have stopped my sensual energies from flowing outwards. But as soon as I retain that energy, it swells in the psyche just as the water which is trapped in a valley or low spot after being restricted by an engineer.

The engineer must have some plan to reinforce the containment. He must have a viaduct to release the energy in a controlled manner. In addition to a strong dam, he must also have a regulated outlet or safety release causeway. This sort of release is different from the method of allowing the river to flow in any direction it pleases. If a person dams a river and does not take these steps, then, of course, the river may break away and do even more damage than it would have done had it not been restricted. And this is exactly what happens when one meditates before mastering the containment of sensuality and the concentration of it.

You heard about Buddha. He took up meditation and by all signs, it appeared that he had no superior guidance. However, he was a contemplative genius. His ability may not be acquired by others. We must get superior guidance, otherwise yoga will be an impossibility.

In the advanced stages, one goes a step further, not just to contain the sensual energies, reinforce the containment, and then allow it to flow out through a special outlet but rather, one controls the flow of energy into the reservoir.

Even though initially one sees the waywardness of the river to be the problem, in a more advanced stage, one understands that it is the source of the water which caused the problem. In a river, the water may come from rainfall or melting ice. In either case, if one can control the rain or ice, the problem would be solved. If we can control how the sensual energies are formulated, then the problem would be eliminated. This is exactly the problem: how to control the formulation of the sensual powers which drive us from day to day.

Admittedly a person has to start where he is. No matter how great God is, still I must start where I am. Did you ever gain control over one bad habit or one undesirable character trait? Did you control it for a time and then be impulsively driven by it again?

Sense of Conscience

Within the living being there is a sense of conscience, which is built up over a period of time and which alerts us to antisocial acts. This conscience is a very delicate psychological mechanism. If we ignore it, our spiritual life will be indefinitely postponed.

It is not easy to understand how this sense of conscience is formulated. The spirit is eternal so why should it be concerned with what is right or wrong? If someone is eternal, he cannot be wiped out even if he does something wrong. Thus why should he care? The answer is simple: Irresponsible activities bring misery. Since the soul is eternal, then it follows that it has perpetual liability. Its deeds can be traced. It can be made responsible for activities.

If I am not careful the conscience becomes dulled and ineffective. Subsequently, I proceed with unrighteous, undesirable acts. In many instances the sense of conscience acts as an advisor from within the mind. If I reject the advice, I proceed with irresponsible acts.

The conscience warns, but I may ignore it. I can squelch it.

To reverse this process, I must maintain a keen sensitivity to it.

Piety and Conscience Compared

Piety is closely related to conscience. While the conscience is merely concerned with a good act for its own sake, piety is concerned with benefits. In other words, piety is motivated. Someone might argue, however, that some piety is spontaneous. This is true. When a pious act was prompted by the conscience and there were no preconceptions about it, when it was done spontaneously without plotting, then it is unmotivated. Still, in that case, there will be a return in the future. It is up to the actor to use that benefit magnanimously. Even so, when the return comes, one may not be in the proper frame of mind to act constructively and may misuse the benefit.

There is an example. Once in a past life, I knew a particular lady. In that life she acted as the mother of my body. Due to the affection between us, we became greatly attached to each other. In that past life we both acted piously and helped society, making wholesome contributions to humanity. Then death came. We were separated.

Later on, we met again in this life. However, when we met, both of us suffered from an aberration in memory. We had this feeling that we should be lovers. This is a case of a benefit from a previous piety where providence arranged a re-acquaintance. By the past life, we were again brought together but we misunderstood the affections. Instead of keeping the moral relation in a mother-son affection, it digressed to one of romantic love. Even though the lady was married, our affections were converted into sexual love, in contrast to the past life when there was a caring, commanding interest on her part and a dependent, serving interest on mine. Thus, we considered how to meet as lovers.

Now if my conscience was strong, I would have known instinctively that it was wrong to permit this conversion of the affections. We cannot rely on piety because it will bring positive benefits in the future which we might interpret incorrectly. We had better be supportive of the conscience.

Preparation for Prayer or Meditation

Repeated efforts at prayer, conservation of sensual energy, concentration or meditation, with repeated observations of how the mind works, show the seeker that initially there is an ease within the mind space. Then numerous thoughts occur one after the other. As soon as one thought releases its energy into the intellect, it becomes expended. Then the intellect may abandon it or use it to create more ideas. Once it is expended, another related or unrelated thought is displayed. Can the meditator stop this process of ongoing thought harassment?

In prayer, concentration or meditation, it is not so much what we desire to accomplish but what we actually attain. Since we are not absolute and since many ideas prove impractical, it is more a matter of what we are allowed to do. Thus we need to observe the laws of nature and note how psychic energies operate. If repeatedly, time and time again, one notices that before meditation or prayer, there are many thoughts which require discharge of energy, then why not make a standard procedure to deal with these mental forms before we pray or meditate? If we have to deal with them, because that is the nature of the mind, then why not make it part of the routine to first check and clear these thoughts?

Our discordant way of life weakens meditation and deprives us of peace of mind. A complicated way of life destroys spiritual efforts. A simplification by scaling down desires for dominance, increases the percentage of peace of mind and upgrades the spiritual effort. We need to sort desires, push off ambitions and live simply. A complicated lifestyle is in fact, an exhibition of arrogance. Complication does not allow us to analyze the injury we inflict on ourselves.

Destiny as the Enemy

Subjectively, destiny may be our friend or enemy, all depending on attitude and understanding of the disparities of life. In absoluteness, destiny is our friend only. Still, such a supreme friend is not always appreciated. Destiny imposes discipline but it can also be permissive, hurling any of us on a regrettable course of indulgence.

Will destiny disturb an ascetic? It certainly will. Its disturbances are in the person's interest in the long run. These remind the person of responsibilities. Destiny produces negative consequences which disturb an ascetic. Some of these erase hard-earned progress, but any resentment will slow down advancement. There are negative elements. They have their right to exist, just as I do. Much of the energy that I may put into fighting negative forces, would be better utilized to improve my condition. I should help the world but only when it is my righted duty. Otherwise, whatever I might do, merely adds to the complexity.

Since the mundane life force in the gross and subtle bodies, is a subtle material energy, it can only sponsor spirituality in part. In fact, it will work against the self in part. For survival's sake, it will always divert one's attention to mundane affairs. Still, one should not resent it. Study its functionality and work around it as best you can.

Resentment towards the life force because of its mundane bias does not help spiritual advancement. If we could regulate the soul power and only engage it with the life force when we can constructively use that potency, we would have less impulsiveness. Of course, it requires mystic vision. Most of us cannot see the intellect objectively. Until we can, we cannot curb the mind or curtail haphazard thinking. It is very difficult to curb something one cannot perceive. A shopkeeper may know that a mouse contaminates the foodstuffs but he may never see the rodent and as a result, he may not be able to get rid of it.

A resentment towards the life force or an expectation for the life force to do more than capable, shows only ignorance of the psyche. The key is to distinctly perceive the mind, intellect, life force and the soul. One should free the self from mystic blindness. The mind, intellect, life force and soul are separate objects.

Destiny and Its Wastage of Our Time

In some instances we see that destiny arranges for the wastage of time. For an efficient person, such wastage can be painful. It causes hard feelings, expressions of anger and frustration. However, if one cannot see the past activity which caused the wastage, one can at least reason that due to a past involvement, one is due for the lapse of time. As such, it should be tolerated.

Let us take the example of a slave. Perhaps his entire life is wasted, serving a master. The slave is not allowed to pursue his interest. He can only look on while others fulfill desires. His time is used up in another's service. Nonetheless, he can be patient with destiny. He can reason that due to some irresponsible activity he was put into that disagreeable position. When the reaction runs its course, he will be freed, provided he does nothing to extend the inconvenience.

The time spent serving another is clocked precisely. Whenever we find ourselves in such a position, we should understand that it is timed exactly. Time cannot be wasted beyond what is due by destiny. It is like a prison term. Usually the captive is released as soon as the sentence runs its course. Even in cases where there is a delay, that is timed by destiny.

No human agency can hold us beyond the allotted span created by the resultant destiny. There is another aspect, however. This is the aspect of a causeless wastage of our time. We must tolerate even those wastages which are not traceable to past irresponsible acts. Destiny has every right to waste our time if it so desires. Difficulties and inconveniences do not take away our time. In fact, these aspects can only take what is rightfully the time of someone else. We feel inconvenienced because we think it is our time. As soon as you release yourself from that idea, the irritation ceases.

Breaking Bad Habits

Impulsiveness comes from the life force in the body. This life force also exists in a subtle form as an energizing gas known in Sanskrit as *prana*. It may be a surprise to know that most of us are controlled by this energizing gas. Why should a person be controlled by a gas? Actually, we are controlled to a greater degree by what we ingest as food and breath. Air is more frequently used than food, yet we ignore our consumption of air. Additionally, the tendency to scramble for food is dictated to us by the life force.

To protect us from its impulsions, we are endowed with an intellect. The intellect is known in Sanskrit by the term *buddhi*. There is a particular discipline for curbing this *buddhi*. It is *buddhi* yoga, which is for controlling the spinning action of the intellect, a rotating organ in the head of the subtle body.

The *buddhi* is an organ in the subtle body just as the pituitary gland is an organ in the brain. If I told you that the brain was a series of changing thoughts, you would feel that I was not speaking in a scientific way. What the brain does for a function and what the brain is as an organ, are two different things. For instance, a hammer is used to drive nails, but a hammer is neither the driving action nor the nails. The driving force travels through the hammer into the nails. Similarly, the thinking action is neither the intellect nor the self which observes the conclusions.

The intellect is a spinning light in the head of the subtle body. From this spinning light and the life force energy, the chakras or energy-gyrating centers in the head of the subtle form, have emerged. In addition, the various mystic sensual perceptions like clairvoyance, clairaudience, telescoping and so on, come from certain particular uses of the intellect. Intelligence or intuition is derived when the soul uses the intellect for interpreting sensual information.

In the yoga system, the process of *pratyāhāra*, withdrawal of sensual concerns, is aimed at stabilizing or slowing down the spinning action of the intellect. The process of *dhāranā*, concentration or focus, is meant to train the intellect to pursue higher objectives. The process of *dhyāna*, contemplation, is meant to slow the intellect to a halt, to stop its spinning action so that the soul can perceive higher dimensions.

Unless one controls the life force, one cannot control the intellect. As soon as one tries to control the intellect, the life force goads it for contrary actions. Before mastering sense withdrawal, one is supposed to master breath regulation, but some say that such practice is just a breathing exercise. They are wrong. If one does not master breath regulation, one cannot master sensual energy withdrawal and higher psyche control. The reason is this: So long as the life energy is not controlled, it will undermine any effort to control the intellect.

Let us assume that we plan to depart in a jet plane. Our objective is to go to another country. First of all, we need to make sure that the engine is in working order. We should have sufficient fuel. We need to be sure that the crew and passengers board the aircraft. Let us assume that we have everything as far as our knowledge permits. We believe that everything is in order. The pilot fires the engines and operates the controls. The plane is airborne. Once airborne, the crew and passengers relax. They are confident about arrival at the destination. However the pilot notices that his fuel gauge registers only a quarter of a tank. He will need an entire tank to get to the destination. He alerts us. What should we do? Should we tell him to proceed regardless? Or should he return to the starting point?

Similarly, in the process of yoga, in the spiritual disciplines, if we neglect essential practice, we will have to stop at some stage, turn about, and learn it, either in this life or in the next. If we advance through higher stages and find that we lack certain skills, just as the aircraft lacked fuel, we should to take an action to develop the required technique.

By using the buddhi intellect organ in the head of the subtle body to institute and enforce constructive traits, an ascetic can train the life force to break bad habits. The buddhi or intellect organ should patiently and repeatedly train the life energy until it adopts the new habits permanently. In addition, the intellect should supervise the life force's intake of energy. If this supervision is lax, the effort to change a habit will be unsuccessful since the life force will then assume the correct habit only some of the time and it will revert to its old pattern the rest of the time.

The Material World

The material forms we view are manifestations of the material energy, but these are surcharged with spiritual power in varying degrees. The material situation, though gross, is based on spiritual reality. A particular form may be more flimsy than another, more unreal; but everything is based on spiritual reality.

From time to time, one may see a supernatural or spiritual being. Some go through their spiritual life, just believing and never seeing any of these directly. On November the 25th of 1996, I was in a deep meditation, contemplating the material energy, trying to see how it is related to the spirits. For those spirits who are repeatedly taking birth in the gross world, the relation with material nature is ongoing, definite, and recurring, so much so that if any of us takes to spiritual life, we cannot help but regard the material world as a necessity. Instead of endeavoring to be transferred to a dimension outside of this world, we work to establish a divine kingdom on earth. We are so bound up in material nature, that we cannot imagine anything more substantial. From this attachment to matter, the idea of divine material bodies emerged.

Calming Nerves / Retracting Energy from Nerves

This is a *pratyāhāra* or sensuality withdrawal technique. Try to relocate the self at the back of the head as shown in the diagram. This would mean pulling the core-self away from its usually centralized position in the brain. Once the core-self is relocated, it will endeavor to return to its usual position, but it should be held in the back of the head at this place where the nervous energies subside. This can be done in a yogic posture or while sitting on a chair or even while the body reclines.

Core-self in centralized position

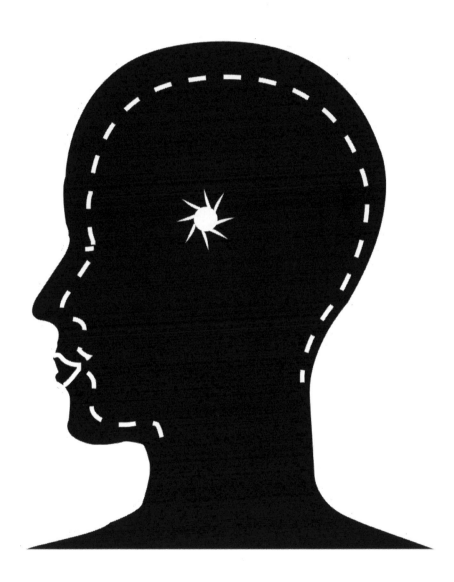

Core-self relocated to back of head

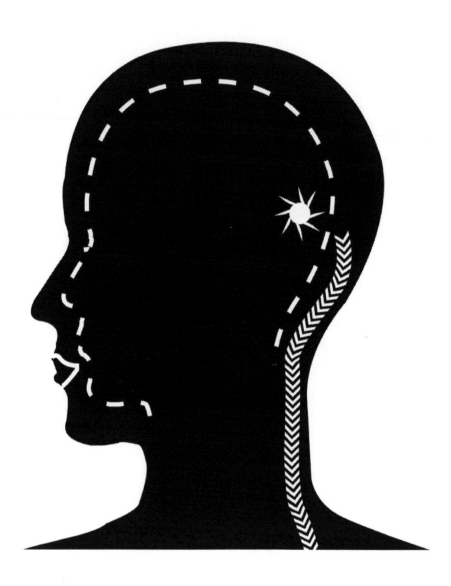

Lalāta Cakra

The *lalāta* chakra is at the top curve of the forehead. It can be seen *easily early in the morning in a dark place just after rising from bed. If one* looks up to see it, it will disappear but if one keeps the eyes looking downwards in the dark, one may see its white or yellow flickering action above in the forehead.

Apart from this, it was revealed to me by Yogeshwarananda *Yogirāj* that this chakra is part of the buddhi intellect organ.

Lalāta chakra perceived as an extension of the intellect

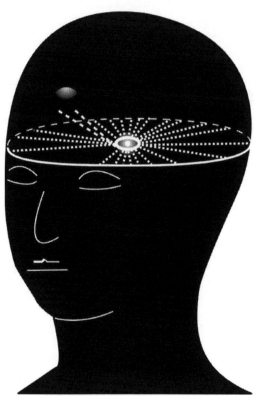

In the diagram above the intellect light is not represented, the core-self is indicated. While perceiving this, one is usually oblivious of the intellect which is positioned between the core-self and the *lalāta* flickering chakra. Since during this perception one does not see the intellect it was not represented but it is present there as an invisible organ between the core-self and the *lalāta* chakra.

Yogeshwarananda showed that nearly all the subtle lights seen or perceived in the head of the subtle body, are emanating from the buddhi organ which is in the mind environment of the subtle form. From the materialistic perspective, the mind and intelligence are just a type of conscious energy, but in actuality the mind is a chamber of mental space. The intellect is an organ flickering in that space.

Here are some diagrams which may help one to distinguish between the mind and the intellect. Just as the skull is an encasement for the brain, the mind is an energy field which contains the buddhi organ.

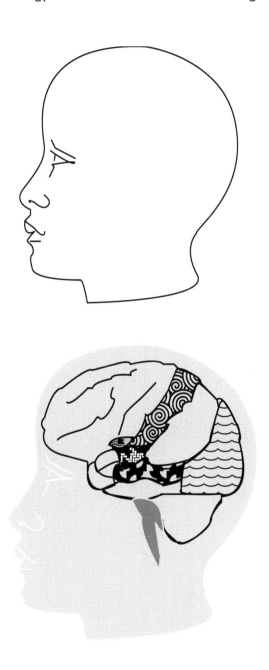

Here the skull is surrounded by an indistinct psychic energy.

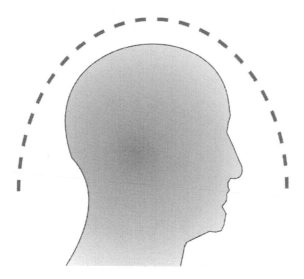

When the buddhi intellect is operating, the mind field shrinks, becoming tense and distinct.

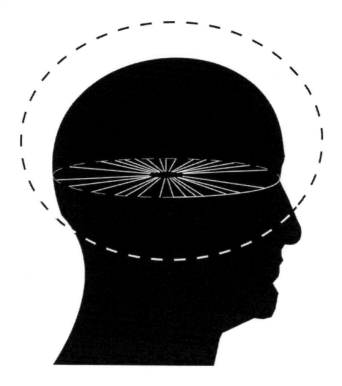

When the buddhi detects a sense object or if the life force senses one, the buddhi flickers quickly to absorb the information it can derive from the object. This causes anxiety. From the materialistic perspective, this detecting action is good but from the perspective of higher yoga, it is unwanted. Hence, in the second verse of his *Yoga Sūtra*, *Patañjali* alerts us to the danger:

- *The skill of yoga is demonstrated by the conscious non-operation of the vibrational modes of the mento-emotional energy. (Yoga Sūtra 1.2)*

The stoppage of ideas is interpreted by some as just a stoppage of thinking. Others say it is a stoppage of sensual pursuits. In yoga practice, it means that the intellect organ stops flickering or stops detecting subtle or gross objects. It becomes unresponsive to mundane vibrations.

Since this body was in infancy, the buddhi organ in the subtle body was very perceptive but I did not understand its operations. I went to many teachers, and I regret to inform that most of these persons were fakes. To their credit, they were religious, godly, saintly or sincere but they had little mystic experience and still they lectured or spoke on mystic matters. Understandably, if a man feels a leadership tendency, what else can he do but lead, even if he does not qualify for giving supervision?

Since infancy, I used to see the flickering, non-yellowish, non-bluish, crystalline light especially in the dark, early in the morning. It is just like a miner's forehead light except that it flickers in the head. The light goes outward in all directions as it rotates like the emergency light on a police car. I used to wonder about that light. I searched and searched through yoga books. Gradually I got a hint that it was the *lalāta* cakra. I knew that it was not the brow cakra because it is higher in the forehead. One yogi, *Swāmī* Sachidananda, said it was the *lalāta* cakra. Later on, however, Śrīla Yogeshwarananda showed me that it is just the intellect flickering around in the head of the subtle body.

This *lalāta* cakra is in the top part of the head. All the living creatures have it, even animals and insects. Wherever we detect some intelligence, it is present. Still, due to its subtlety most of us cannot perceive it.

The direction of rotation of the *lalāta* cakra and of the intellect is shown in the next diagram. This is according to my experience. It rotates swiftly like a helicopter rotor. One sees it turning at a very high speed. It appears to rotate in an anti-clockwise direction.

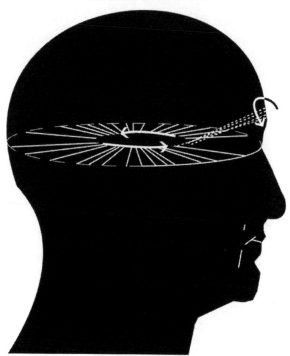

Pratyāhāra Sensual Withdrawal

A very important aspect of yoga is sensual energy withdrawal. Every spiritual group uses some type of sensual restraint. *Pratyāhāra* means the complete withdrawal of sensual powers from the material world. It is the removal of interest in exploiting the various phases of the material energy. These exploitive tendencies come out of the causal body but most of us do not know the causal form. Sometimes when someone says "*me*" or "*I*", one or both hands naturally go to the central chest area.

This is an indication of the causal body's location. It is a subtle dimension. *Pratyāhāra* means that our sensual interest is being withdrawn. It is a difficult and unnatural feat. Which of us can honestly and truly say we are finished with everything in this world? So long as we maintain just a slight interest, the whole world is exposed and the sensual energies are liable to start pouring out impulsively.

Sensual withdrawal begins by pulling in the senses that you are most prone to using. Usually this is the visual sense. If, however, you have a more predominant sense, then retract that one. Suppose you use the ear more than the eye, as in the case of a blind man; then begin by pulling in your hearing energy.

All the energies must be recalled, either collectively or singly. Each must be isolated, identified and retracted. There are several strands of sensual interest which must be withdrawn for sense control. Some of these are: visual sense, hearing sense, touching sense, tasting sense, smelling sense, food absorption sense, and sex energy expression sense.

After years of practice, I found that in advanced levels when one mastered the sensual retraction, the energy reverses direction into the psyche and takes the shape of a ball. Here is a series of diagrams:

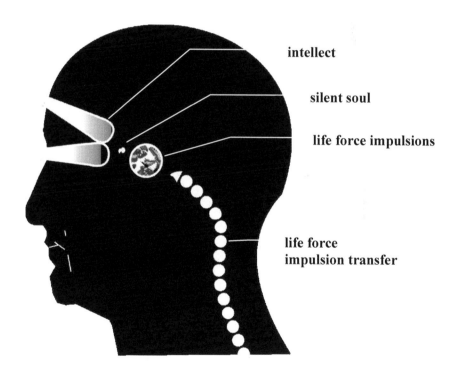

intellect

silent soul

life force impulsions

**life force
impulsion transfer**

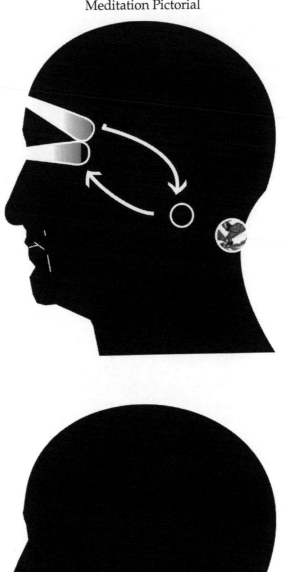

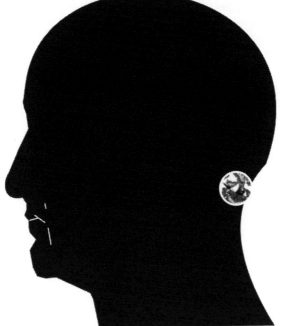

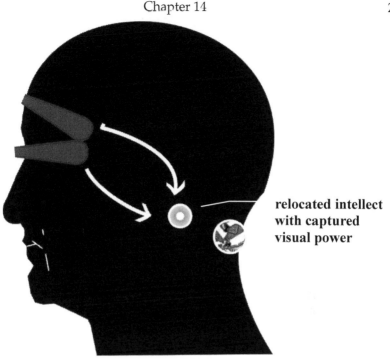

**relocated intellect
with captured
visual power**

An Open-Eye Meditation

Persons who are now beginning to meditate, should do so in private, with eyes closed either in subdued light or darkness. In the beginning, one needs to find the best circumstance under which one can quiet the mind. Quieting the mind is not meditation but it is preliminary. As soon as the mind is quieted, many dormant ideas burst as mental sounds and images. These, expand into visions, schemes and daydreams. For most people, the attempt at meditation becomes a struggle with haphazard mental activity and random emotions. Some give up in frustration, admitting, "I simply cannot meditate."

If the eyes are open, the mind becomes distracted. Thus the eyes should be closed. Some yogis recommend half-closed eyes. Fully-closed eyes are best for beginners because they are fatigued by the sensations which enter an open eyelid. In addition, a beginner will get better results if the meditation is done in the dark or in subdued light. Bright light stimulates brain nerves, triggers the mind, and activates the intellect organ.

One important aspect is location. Many ancient yogis who practiced, lived in caves or at least in isolation. Why caves? In caves, direct light is absent. The brain nerves settle down. The external stimuli are absent. Since we do not have caves, what should we do? Actually, many of us retire to cave-like rooms.

What we require is ample ventilation without bright light. Modern rooms may have inadequate air-flow. One method is to leave the windows and/or doors open while covering the head with a dark cotton cloth, but this is not suitable in cold climates. One may lie, recline, or sit up in the yoga posture. It is said that one cannot meditate unless his spine is vertically erect and his body is in a cross-legged posture. But this statement applies to those with supple limbs. Others can meditate while lying down. One cannot meditate in a yoga posture unless the body is relaxed in that position. Any strain will attract the life force and the mind. These will in turn, activate the intellect. Once the intellect is alerted, the meditation will cease. Thus one who is not proficient in postures may meditate while sitting on a chair, while reclining, or by lying down.

I was taught a procedure by a Shiva Deity for meditating with my eyes wide open. This procedure is advanced. Once I was in a staff meeting at my work place. It was time for a routine meditation. Suddenly, a Shiva Deity spoke within my consciousness. He said, "Send your attention down into the heart cove. Initially do not try to enter. Meditate on the energy that flows out of the vent. Keep your eyes open so as not to draw attention from others."

The vent tube mentioned is a tube that comes from the causal cove, the causal body. The following diagram shows that tube.

Conclusion

As one journeys through life, the opportunity for meditation and the resulting spiritual advancement is ever-present while, at the same time, remaining elusive amidst the barrage of mundane influences. Take time out of your day to meditate, even if for only a few minutes. Share your successes and frustrations with others and learn from those who are positioned to help you at your particular level of development.

The positive results of a steady practice will manifest and will assist you greatly throughout life, at the moment of death, and in the afterlife.

Index

About Author

Michael Beloved (Madhvacharya das) took his current body in 1951 in Guyana. In 1965, while living in Trinidad, he instinctively began doing yoga postures and trying to make sense of the supernatural side of life.

Later on, in 1970, in the Philippines, he approached a Martial Arts Master named Mr. Arthur Beverford, explaining to the teacher that he was seeking a yoga instructor; Mr. Beverford identified himself as an advanced disciple of Sri Rishi Singh Gherwal, an ashtanga yoga master.

Mr. Beverford taught the traditional ashtanga Yoga with stress on postures, attentive breathing and brow chakra centering meditation. In 1972, Michael entered the Denver Colorado Ashram of Kundalini Yoga Master Sri Harbhajan Singh. There he took instruction in Bhastrika Pranayama and its application to yoga postures. He was supervised mostly by Yogi Bhajan's disciple named Prem Kaur.

In 1979 Michael formally entered the disciplic succession of the Brahma-Madhava Gaudiya Sampradaya through Swami Kirtanananda, who was a prominent sannyasi disciple of the Great Vaishnava Authority Sri Swami Bhaktivedanta Prabhupada, the exponent of devotion to Sri Krishna.

For producing this publication, Michael took instructions from many yogi mystics on the astral planes. For forty years he took notes during meditation practice. This book, among others, details the experiences.

Made in the USA
Charleston, SC
22 January 2010